Federico Fellini

Francesco Tornabene

Federico Fellini

The Fantastic Visions of a Realist

Benedikt Taschen

© 1990 Benedikt Taschen Verlag GmbH
Otto-Suhr-Allee 59, D-1000 Berlin 10

Graphic design: Detlev Schaper, Cologne
Cover design: Peter Feierabend, Berlin
English translation: Melanie Richter-Bernburg

Printed in West Germany
ISBN 3-89450-154-5

Contents

Foreword

The Maestro summons his faces using a simple but effective device, an advertisement more or less like the following, placed in a newspaper: "Signor Fellini is preparing to make a new film and would be pleased to see all those who would like to meet him."

And there are a lot of people who want to meet him, most of them, of course, in the hope of getting a part, however small, in his new film – just once they would like to be part of the scurrilous universe of Fellini's films. This desire, sometimes almost an obsession, wondrously brings together people of the most different kinds, welding them together for as long as it takes to make the film. Fellini will thus be busy for a while reviewing this never-ending stream of visitors. For him, the parade of faces is the first important step toward the realization of his new project: "I sit behind my desk with brushes and pencils and thousands of people come in. I chat with them a little, do some sketches, ask a few questions, collect photographs. For me this is the most exciting part. It's like having a film come to me, like a film in tiny fragments, here a smile, there a glance, a pair of socks, a bit of dialogue, or just the way a person lights a cigarette."[1] Like a benevolent vampire Fellini extracts cinematographic elixir from everything he sees, and in his drawings he captures the spirits of the figures he has created. It is, as he admits, the part of his work that gives him the greatest pleasure. What interests him most are the faces of his visitors, for Fellini assigns his roles by physiognomy. He doesn't want people to act in his films; what he wants is an authentic embodiment of the creatures of his imagination.

People who want to find out more about Fellini's figures, most of them absurdly exaggerated, or about the Maestro himself usually need a lot of patience and, even more importantly, strong nerves. Fellini hates interviews – at least that's what he always says. But that doesn't keep him from giving them constantly. You have to watch out for his interviews, though, because he doesn't always tell the truth: "I am a liar," he says, "but an honest one."[2] And a capricious one at that: if he says something once, you shouldn't be surprised if he takes it back in his next interview and suddenly expresses what seem to be quite different opinions. He doesn't want to be pinned down; even more than that, he "wants to be able to make a mistake" – because making mistakes is, after all, human, and that's very important to Fellini. Asking his advice is sometimes a necessity though, because his films have become more and more subjective with time, and without the director's explanations they are often simply beyond an audience's understanding.

There have been repeated attempts to classify Fellini's work. At the beginning it was regarded as "neorealistic", then as as an example of "poetic realism", later as "baroque". But whatever categories we use, they hardly do justice to it since such terms cannot define it fully. Fellini himself has always rejected the idea of categorizing his films.

But how do you best approach Federico Fellini, especially if you want to write a book about him? Given the complicated picture we have just drawn, it would seem to be very difficult, especially since the things that have been said about the great director are so contradictory. A real dilemma. Fortunately Fellini himself comes to the rescue: "I can't bear people who try to define me too closely!"[3] Perhaps we should content ourselves, then, with an attempt to draw closer to the fascinating personality of Federico Fellini. This doesn't

Fellini at his desk, 1968

mean that we must settle for superficiality it's simply a matter of recognizing that we will never understand the complexity of Fellini as a man and as a director and that the best way to approach him is through his films. Photographs made on the set are also helpful and as many as possible are included here, along with others that show the Maestro at work and in private.

A book such as this one, like any book on films that is not a scholarly study, can only present what the actor Oscar Werner once called the "shadows of our dreams". And Fellini's films are nothing less than the shadows of his dreams. Seeing them means feeling, and feeling means beginning to understand who Federico Fellini really is. For more than almost any other contemporary director, Fellini reveals himself most radically in his films.

Childhood, Youth – Fellini's Way to Film

> "My childhood, my memories, my longings, my dreams – I have invented almost all of them just for the pleasure of telling them to others."[4]

In short, Fellini lies. But we knew that already and he has never denied it. That's just one of the problems you have when you want to describe his life truthfully. Once you begin, though, you are inevitably confronted with yet another difficulty: Fellini is a sorcerer of lies with many apprentices. He himself is largely responsible for the wild and freely-invented stories that circulate about him, having carelessly allowed them to escape from his fantasy and take on form, often on the basis of the experiences of others. But in the course of the years these stories have been joined by the inventions of his apprentices, and Fellini has become ever more bound up in myth and ever less accessible to factual biography. Federico Fellini is both the original and a forgery. Whatever you hear about him, you should be careful not to believe it straight off. But then, you ask, why should you believe me? Did I ever say you could?

> "I don't remember."

Federico Fellini was born on January 20, 1920, in Rimini in the Via le Dardanelli.[5] His father, Urbano Fellini, was a travelling salesman who was born on a farm near Gambettola; he died on May 31, 1956. His mother, Ida Barbiani (who died on September 27, 1984), was from Rome, from a "good" family, as they say. Her parents were wealthy business people whose ancestors, according to Fellini, could be traced back to the 14th century.[6]

Apart from the fragments that can be reconstructed from his films, scarcely anything is known about Fellini's childhood. At any rate, he remains silent on the subject in interviews, or he boldly asserts: "I don't remember my childhood. I invent it when I need it. Maybe I never was a child. I think I became Fellini at the age of 22; before that I was nothing, it was just a long incubation period."[7] Well, that's one way of looking at it: film-making as an incurable disease caused by a memory virus from a time that has been denied. Fellini has been infected by his own childhood and youth. Many of his films are nothing more than bouts of fever resulting from this same illness. That's why it's important to try to form a picture of these early years from the fragments available here and there; most of the myths and visions in his works have their roots in this part of his life.

Fellini's parents were members of the educated bourgeoisie, and his father's work provided the family with financial security. Although his father was frequently away from home, Federico, his brother Riccardo and his sister Maddalena grew up in a family that was intact. His early experiences were dominated by three things: life in the country – or rather, the narrowness of life in the country –, the Catholic Church, and Fascism. What this meant was that Fellini had to subject himself early on to extremely rigid social structures that demanded blind obedience to authority and which regulated everyday life through dogma, ritual and prejudice.

The most intense influence was undoubtedly that exercised by the Church, which was apparently "more Catholic" in Rimini and the surrounding area than it was elsewhere in Italy. Even now the large number of saints revered

The six-year-old Federico with his younger brother Riccardo, 1926

Scene from *8½* with Marcello Mastroianni, 1963

there is an expression of the strong religiosity maintained among the people by the Church. The strong influence of the Catholic Church is also shown, however, by the large number of holidays, whose high point is always a procession.

In areas such as this superstition is often deeply rooted, and witches, faith healers and mysterious events often provide the topics of conversation and stimulate the fantasies of not only the most sensitive souls. It seems likely that Fellini's fascination with magic and the supernatural has its source here. He returns again and again to such things in his life, has astrological, occult and spiritualist phases, shows a great deal of interest in the spiritual techniques and practices of primitive peoples, in yoga and Zen, and has dealings with mediums, sorcerers and fortune tellers.

But even if he says that during his childhood he was aware of "inexplicable occurrences",[8] he doesn't believe all of the unbelievable stories he is told. He just wants to remain open to all the things that can stimulate the imagination: "I'm not interested in the logic of things, their 'comprehensibility'. In fact the things that can least be subjected to the control of the senses, and therefore may seem least real to others, are particularly real to me. That's what fascinates me."[9] There are probably similar reasons for Fellini's fascination with Catholicism, quite apart from the fact that he can't get away from it because of his upbringing, both in the family and by representatives of the Church – for instance, the nuns at the elementary school of San Vincenzo.

"I think I'm religious by nature."

A Catholic figure frequently plays a role in Fellini's films, not seldom as an object of ridicule. Fellini says that he is religious by nature[10] but that he can hardly approve of what the Church has made of Christian teachings. Like many other Italians, he has a love-hate relationship with his faith. On the one hand he likes the Church with all its splendour, its rituals and ceremonies, as a kind of mystic drama, but on the other he is appalled by its dogmatism, especially since he is an enemy of the use of slogans and of any kind of creed or ideology.

Fellini said very tellingly at the beginning of his film career: "I am Catholic, at least from a sociological point of view. I am a product of a Christian milieu. I am typically Italian, steeped in Mediterranean civilization and Western culture. I can't be non-Catholic."[11] At least his first works are to be seen as Christian statements. He was rightfully referred to at the time as a "Christian creator of films", for as Martin Schlappner has said: "His themes revolve around the fundamental questions of Christian belief, man's need for salvation and the healing and redemption of life."[12]

For Fellini man is not only a social being but also and always a divine one as well. That's why people have always fascinated him. Fellini's preference for odd human types probably has its source in the region he came from, Emilia Romagna. These people, especially the ones he met during his summer vacations at his grandmother's in Gambettola, reappear in the unusual physiognomy of his cinematic descriptions. Nowadays we would call these figures Felliniesque.

Scene with Bruno Zanin as Titta in *Amarcord*, 1973

"Madonna or Whore."

But there were other sources for myths in Fellini's childhood and some of them are related to three events that should be described in greater detail here. The first has to do, albeit indirectly, with the Church. We already know that as a small boy Federico went to an elementary school run by Vincentian nuns. A lay sister at the school made a great impression upon him. In the marathon interview he gave to the Italian film critic Giovanni Grazzini, Fellini talked about his experience: "How old that buxom girl might have been I don't know, probably somewhere between 15 and 20. I only remember that she put her arms around me from time to time and pressed me against her, rubbed me up against her, surrounded by the smell of potato peels, the odour of rancid meat broth and the typical smell of nuns' habits. One day, when she was rubbing me up against her big, strong, warm body like a little Pinocchio, I felt a longing, a tickling feeling in the tip of my nose that I couldn't understand but which was so pleasurable that I nearly fainted. I think that must have been my first experience of sexual arousal for even now I grow weak when I smell potato peels."[13]

Beyond its culinary and erotic aspects, this adventure seems to have awakened Fellini's liking for generous female forms. A second and perhaps

Scene from *8½*, 1963

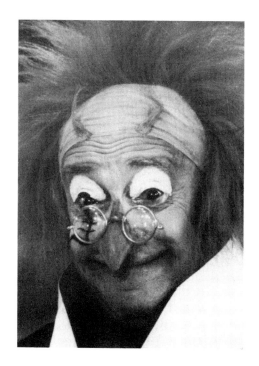

Clown in *The Clowns,* 1970

central experience in his childhood may have been the more immediate source of his weakness for dimensions à la Rubens. The encounter was with a prostitute. The woman's name was Saraghina and she lived in a hut on the beach at Rimini. For a bit of small change she would give a kind of open-air peep show and, at the age of eight, Federico took part in such an event along with some older boys: "Trembling, I stopped a few steps away from Saraghina, close enough to take in the smell of her, a mixture of algae, fish, tobacco, decaying wood, and oil. Saraghina counted her money, gave us a sharp glance and, as the sky turned purple, began the ritual. With a solemn gesture, a mixture of respect for herself and for us, she showed herself slowly a number of times. Then she turned her back to us and repeated her revealing movements. An unbelievably gigantic white mass, a kind of Moby Dick, but she didn't frighten me, although I couldn't say a word to my friends for more than a quarter of an hour afterwards. Later on, I played hookey from school one day to see this disturbing mythical creature again. She sang the 'Hazel Nut Rhumba' in a penetrating, smokey voice. I said 'Hello. What a nice voice you have!' And then I went away, waving my sailor's cap in farewell."[14] The experience positively cries out to be filmed. And Fellini did exactly that in 1963, the lay sister on the one hand, the prostitute on the other – two confusing poles. A child on a voyage of discovery, and what remained was a distorted image of women. How else can we understand a statement like the following one, made by the adult Fellini: "It's terribly difficult for a man to see a woman properly – she's either a Madonna or a whore."[15] We could say that this represents a banal and oversimplified psychological interpretation of the adventure; even if that is the case, the encounter still has a certain symbolic character, for Fellini's memories of the time following elementary school are full of women like Saraghina. Fellini and women! A subject in its own right – but we'll take a closer look at this later.

"I tell stories about the circus in all my films."[16]

The third event that made a lasting impression on the boy Federico and on his dreams was his first encounter with the world of the circus. In the

Scene from *Amarcord,* 1973

12

interview with Grazzini Fellini says: "I still remember that I felt something like an exciting, prophetic and anticipatory resonance the first time I set foot in the calm, damp breath of the huge belly of a circus tent. I felt at home in the enchanted void – the damp sawdust, the sound of the hammer, dull noises from somewhere in the background, the neighing of a horse... It was the Pierino Circus that I told about in *The Clowns*. It was probably tiny, but it seemed huge to me, like a spaceship, a hot air balloon I would like to have sailed off in."[17] Fellini has never lost this desire and it is not without reason that he says all his films are basically about the circus. But we can talk about that in more detail later, too.

"To make up for my own emptiness, I turned to art."

If we read Fellini's rare comments on his school days, it comes as no surprise that they are full of descriptions of different types of people. While we may recall our fear of an exam or our dislike of a certain teacher, Fellini remembers women with enormous breasts and hips, or his eyes light up with the memory of an eccentric. To a certain extent he even describes himself as an eccentric.

There is his mention, for instance, of a slim Federico who looked like a girl in photographs and who was given the nickname "Ghandi" in high school. He must have suffered a great deal because of his appearance and in the summer he didn't dare appear on the beach in swimming trunks: "I lived a secluded and lonely life. I looked to famous models, Leopardi above all, to justify my dislike of swimming trunks, my inability to enjoy splashing around in the water like all the others (maybe the sea is still so fascinating for me because I never conquered it – it's still the place monsters and spirits come from). In any case, to make up for my own emptiness I turned to art."[18]

Fellini remembered his love of comic books and developed the penchant for drawing he had already shown as a small child. His efforts in this direction went so far that he opened an art shop with an older friend in the summer of 1937. They called their shop "Phoebus" and drew caricatures and portraits on commission. At the beginning their only clients were society women, but after the two draughtsmen had made a name for themselves they expanded their scope. Fellini finally came to draw caricatures of movie stars from the

Scene from *The Young and the Passionate*, 1953

films running at the Fulgor in Rimini and the hand-coloured drawings were exhibited in showcases outside the cinema. Fellini's first contact with the cinema had been made. The payment for his art work took the form of free tickets to the shows and they were quickly used up for trips to the cinema with his friends.

At the Fulgor, almost legendary itself for the little erotic adventures that took place there, Fellini liked to watch comedies. He discovered his preference for this genre early on, and if you ask him about his models he usually mentions actors that fascinated him at that time: the Marx brothers, for instance, or Laurel and Hardy and Buster Keaton. Under the Fascists scarcely any other films were permitted anyway; and when they were, they were "clean" – politically speaking.

The dream machine of the cinema was brightly polished. This was the "white telephone" era, so-called for the film *White Telephones* by Dino Risi. Life in these films was uncomplicated and wonderful. But this didn't bother Fellini and his friends. Along with the rest of the audience they just wanted a laugh – nothing wrong with that, especially if times are bad.

We could rightly ask where Fellini found the time during his school years for all of his other activities, especially since he also enjoyed doing sweet nothing with his friends. (In *The Young and the Passionate* [*I vitelloni*, 1953] and in *Amarcord* [1973] he gives cinematic treatment to this aspect of his youth.) The answer is simple: he often simply skipped school. And he admits to having learned very little in school; at most it was the place where he started training his powers of observation. Nothing that could be used later for the purposes of caricature escaped his sharp eyes. Fellini loved this activity, so far removed from instruction but so close to life. He decided to make it his profession.

"I didn't know what a script was yet."

While he was still in grammar school he began sending the fruits of his observations to various newspapers in the form of caricatures, jokes, stories and novellas. The *Domenica del Corriere* was the first to publish anything by Fellini.[19] On February 6, 1938, a small caricature appeared among the contributions by readers. This was an encouragement to Fellini to keep trying. He tenaciously submitted his texts and drawings and finally encountered Giuseppe Nerbini in Florence. Nerbini, who published several humorous weeklies, was the next in a long line of publishers for whom Fellini would work on a more or less regular basis.

In 1938, with his school leaving certificate in his pocket, Fellini began to work directly for several of Nerbini's publications, e.g. for *Il 420*, a satiric newspaper, and for *L'Avventuroso*, which published American comics almost exclusively. At first Fellini's job consisted of reading proof for the publications. Later on, when the Fascist government prohibited the importation and publication of foreign newspapers and journals, he wrote but didn't draw for a comic strip series that retained already established figures: "I knew all of the figures by heart, the planet Mongo and its emperor Ming. I knew intuitively which adventure Guy L'eclair and his companions would encounter. I didn't have the feeling I was working. It was simply fun to invent ever more daring adventures for the cartoonists. I didn't know what a script was yet. I made up a story, wrote the dialogue and divided it up among the eight or twelve pictures of each plate."[20] In a sense Fellini was busy collecting his first experience as a director. But he would express his love of comics only later in film, in his first independently realized project, *The White Sheik (Lo sceicco bianco)* (1952).

Street scene from *Fellini's Roma*, 1971

"Rome is my private flat."

In January 1939 Fellini went to Rome, partly because of his parents, who were urging him to go to university: "My father wanted to make a lawyer of me at all costs, while my mother couldn't decide between a doctor and a bishop. Although I knew that I wouldn't become a lawyer or a doctor, let alone a bishop, I enrolled in the school of law at the university. That is, I had a friend enroll me, because I never set foot in a lecture hall."[21]

In spite of what has sometimes been said, Fellini is therefore not a lawyer, and his doctorate is an honorary one. Instead of pursuing his studies, he went to every newspaper and journal in Rome, offering to work for them. He wanted to be a journalist. He had always been impressed by the reporters in American films: "I liked their coats and the way they wore their hats pushed back on their heads."[22]

Fellini was lucky in Rome. Shortly after his arrival he began to freelance for various newspapers and magazines, among them one on film. (There are highly amusing episodes in *Intervista* based on his work for this magazine.) But Fellini did not limit himself to merely journalistic work. Besides his reports, interviews and feature stories, he wrote gags and sketches for the radio and short scenes for variety theatre. He wrote dialogue for comic books, created advertising slogans and leaflets and, with a friend, painted the windows of various shops with advertising. But this still wasn't enough for the energetic Fellini. He often worked his way through pubs and restaurants in the evening, drawing portraits and caricatures for paying customers as he went.

During this phase Fellini led the life of a vagabond. He changed flats several times a month, "either because I couldn't pay the rent or because there were

Scene from *Variety Lights,* 1950

romantic complications with the landlady"[23], and very shortly he knew his way around all of Rome. The premonition he had etperienced on arriving in the city thus came true: "I had scarcely arrived in Rome when I had the feeling I belonged there. Now I see Rome as my private flat."[24]

During this nomadic period in his life the industrious vagabond met many people. One of them was the famous comedian Aldo Fabrizi, who was appearing in variety shows at the time and who later achieved international recognition for his role as the priest in Rossellini's film *Roma, città aperta* (1945). In the summer of 1939 Fellini interviewed Fabrizi for *Cine Magazzino*; it was the beginning of a long friendship. Fabrizi took an interest in the 18-year-old Fellini and introduced him to the world of variety theatre. Fellini expressed his thanks by supplying Fabrizi with ideas and gags for his appearances. The friendship led to professional co-operation between the two after Fabrizi made a name for himself in films as well as in variety. Fellini wrote the screenplays for some of Fabrizi's films, for example *Avanti, c'e posto* (1942) and *L'ultima carrozzella* (1943). For a project with the title *Emigranti*, which was never realized, Fellini not only wrote the script, but was supposed to co-direct it with Fabrizi.[25]

The experience Fellini gathered in variety theatre, especially during Fabrizi's career, was used by the director later on when he made *Variety Lights* (*Luci del varietà*) in 1950 with Alberto Lattuada. But it is still 1939, the middle of spring, and Fellini has just succeeded in securing the job of editorial secretary with the popular satirical journal *Marc'Aurelio*. Even now he is quite proud of this accomplishment for, as he says, when he was in grammar school *Marc'Aurelio* was "mythic", "one of those forbidden gifts, shrouded in mystery, that reached us from wonderful, dreamlike Rome, where the films of Fred Astaire and Jean Harlow came to us from an unreal America, from an Atlantis we could only dream of. Buying and reading *Marc'Aurelio* had the same forbidden charm as smoking in secret or trying to sneak into a bordello on the coat-tails of a friend who was already of age."[26]

Fellini rapidly became one of the most creative, productive and popular members of the staff of the magazine, and he soon filled the different rubrics

Stage scene from *Variety Lights* with Giulietta Masina, et al., 1950

Giulietta Masina and Peppino de Filippo in *Variety Lights*, 1950

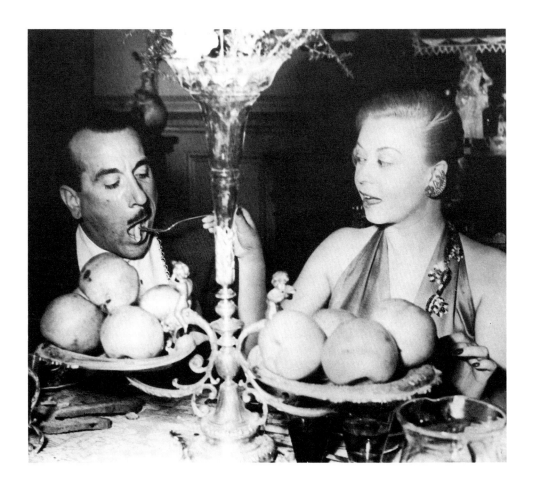

Giulietta Masina and Peppino de Filippo in *Variety Lights*, 1950

for which he wrote and drew with the same arsenal of Felliniesque figures that were later to dominate his films. He continued to work for the radio and finally succeeded in finding his way into films through a colleague at *Marc' Aurelio*. This helpful colleague was Stefano Vanzina, who is now better known under the pseudonym of Steno as director of Bud Spencer films. Vanzina gave Fellini a chance to write gags for Mario Mattoli, who made a number of films with Erminio Macario in the 30's and 40's. The assembly-line style of production meant there was a constant need for new people and new ideas. Fellini, who was simply bubbling over with ideas, came along just at the right moment. He was involved in the writing of scripts for *Imputato alzatevi!* (1939) – which was never made –, for *Lo vedi come sei* (1939) and for *Non me lo dire* (1940). Fellini's film debut thus took place through a series of commercially-oriented films of middling quality.

Fellini was only to work as a scriptwriter in his own right later on, after meeting Piero Tellini, when he was finally able to deliver more than just the jokes for stories other writers had invented. In co-operation with Tellini, who had already made a name for himself as a scriptwriter, Fellini co-wrote the screenplays for *Documento zeta 3* (1941), *Quarta pagina* (1942), *Avanti c'e posto* (1942) – where Fellini appeared in the credits for the first time[27] –, *Chi l'ha visto* (1942), *Campo de fiori* (1942) and *I predoni del Sahara* (1942). The latter was to be filmed on location in Africa under the direction of Gino Talamo, but during the filming problems developed and Fellini had to fly to Africa to make necessary changes in the script. When Talamo had to give up work on the film as a result of an automobile accident an attempt was made to get Fellini to take over as director.[28] Fellini agreed immediately, but filming was never completed since Italian and German troops in Africa had to fall back from their positions following the landing of American forces. Filming turned out to be too dangerous under these conditions and the whole team thus returned to Italy. The project was never completed.

"I was even in an insane asylum for three days."

Up to this point Fellini had been able to avoid being drafted into the army, first as a student, later on by pointing to the fact that he was a journalist. When these excuses no longer worked, he bribed doctors to declare him unfit for active service[29] or he simulated heart ailments or Basedow's disease.[30] But that wasn't all: "I was even in an insane asylum for three days in my underwear with a towel on my head like a maharajah. Then the Italian military doctors were replaced by Germans, and the end of my repeatedly extended recovery period, which had kept me out of things for three years, appeared to be inevitable. A German who looked like a drunk handed me a stack of forms and said I was to report to my regiment in Greece 'immediatelyandatonce' (as he said). I understood that I was to hurry, but just as he said 'at once' all hell broke loose. The Americans bombed Bologna and the hospital was hit. I took off like a shot, without my shoes and covered with limestone and dust... since that day I haven't heard another word about my orders to report."[31] As is the case with a number of other events in Fellini's life, there are various versions of how he managed to avoid being sent to the front in Greece. The one reported by Tullio Kezich in his Fellini biography would seem to be the most credible, not so much because it sounds realistic – exactly the opposite is the case! – but because Kezich's book was so carefully researched. We can assume that Kezich describes things as they were: Fellini, who became eligible for duty in 1939, managed to find one excuse after the other until October 29, 1943, when he was caught by the authorities and turned over to the German military.

During transport to his company, he managed to escape: "He saved himself by means of an impudent trick, a real Fellini 'gag,' by acting as if he recognized an officer of the Wehrmacht on the Via del Babuino. He jumped down from the truck and called 'Fritz! Fritz!', waved and then embraced the puzzled German, ending the farce with a gesture of apology. In the meantime, though, the truck had driven off. The officer didn't understand a thing, and Federico disappeared..."[32]

Fellini was able to return to his multimedia activities unharmed, and he turned first to the development of a series for radio. Here he drew on two figures he had invented for *Marc'Aurelio*, Cipo and Pallina, names that were also used as the title for the series broadcast weekly on radio. It was about a young couple and was so popular among listeners that a producer wanted to film a number of the segments. Unfortunately these plans were never realized, but there were other and more important developments for Fellini.

"Pallina, will you marry me?"

Fellini, who knew only the voices of "his" couple, was curious about the people behind them. First he made an agreement to meet with Cipo, but this meeting must have been quite a disappointment. Grown cautious, he called the young, blonde actress from Bologna who was the voice of Pallina. Her name was Giulietta Masina and she was studying modern literature. If the content of the telephone conversation has been reported correctly, Fellini said: "Hello, Pallina, my name is Fellini. I'm tired of life, but before I die, I want to see what my heroine looks like."[33]

The heroine was evidently also curious about her author and a meeting actually did take place. It was followed by a number of others, and legend has it that Fellini one day sent his Pallina two young geese wearing name tags around their necks. One was called Pallina, the other Federico, and in a letter accompanying the unusual gift he asked: "Pallina, will you marry me?

Federico Fellini with wife Giulietta Masina, 1958

Scene with Carla del Poggio in *Variety Lights*, 1950

Federico. P.S. I have sent an answer form along for the sake of simplicity. You only have to sign and return it."[34]

The wedding took place on October 30, 1943, after an engagement of nine months.

"A Wild West general store complete with brawls."

Rome was a city dominated by need and unemployment following the liberation by American troops in June 1944. Although for many Italians this was the beginning of a time of privation, Fellini, whose inventiveness had always earned him good money, was able to keep himself and his wife above water. Along with some friends from *Marc'Aurelio* he opened The Funny Face Shop. Here American soldiers could have portraits, photographs and caricatures made of themselves or could cut records. "It was a Wild West general store complete with scuffles and brawls", Fellini says. "They always arrived dead drunk and started grabbing the girls. For the sake of chivalry we'd sometimes have to intervene, and then the craziest things would happen. Fortunately the shop was on the Via Nazionale, across from the Palazzo delle Esposizioni where the military police had taken up headquarters. One of us would always stand guard and then run across the street to call the MP's. They would come and start banging on anyone within reach and then we'd have to close for a day or two."[35]

Fellini never tires of saying that he has never earned as much money as he did with the Funny Face Shop. And he may even be right, for after just two weeks, the first branch shop opened, and within six months there were nine such shops in Rome. Branches were planned for all over Italy, but the fact that Fellini's Funny Face empire didn't expand any further was the result of an encounter with the director Roberto Rossellini. Rossellini showed up in one of the shops one day and wanted to engage Fellini as the author of a short film about Don Giuseppe Morosini, a priest who had been shot by the Fascists. Although Fellini agreed, he was not entirely convinced of the project at the outset. During the meetings that followed, which included Sergio Amidei as third author along with Fellini and Rossellini, the idea for a short film of a documentary nature underwent great change. What finally emerged was *Roma, città aperta* (1945), a masterly portrayal of the situation of Italy following its defeat in war. Its unvarnished depiction of reality marked the high point of Italian neo-realism. In West Germany the film was a victim of self-imposed censorship until 1961. For years this film, as well as the later *Paisà* (1946) and *Germania, anno zero* (1947/48) by Rossellini, was accused of having "anti-German tendencies"[36].

"I realized that film is probably the most appropriate means of expression for me."

Fellini remained with Rossellini. He closed his Funny Face Shops after the end of the war in 1945 and wrote, again with Amidei, the screenplay for Rossellini's *Paisà*.

The filming of *Paisà*, which tells in moving images of the liberation of Italy, took Fellini on a trip through his own country for the first time. Fellini, who had known only Rimini and Rome up to then, became acquainted with other places and people, and he discovered Italy as an inexhaustible source of inspiration.

As with *Roma, città aperta*, Rossellini took his friend and pupil Fellini as assistant director for *Paisà*. Fellini, acquiring a taste for film-making during his work on the project, began to think about becoming a director himself: "I really came into contact with film for the first time through *Paisà*. I realized that film is probably the most appropriate means of expression for me. Given my laziness, my ignorance, my curiosity about life, my thirst for knowledge, my desire to see everything, to be independent, my lack of discipline and my inability to make real sacrifices, I had the feeling it was the right form of expression for me."[37] This feeling was reinforced by the recognition that "you can also say profound things through film"[38] – something that was always important to Fellini.

During the same year that he made *Paisà*, Fellini met Tullio Pinelli. Pinelli was, like Fellini, Tellini and many other scriptwriters, an admirer of the author and journalist Cesare Zavattini, who can undoubtedly be called the pioneer of neo-realism in Italy (he died in 1989). Zavattini's scripts and theoretical writings made a lasting contribution to Italian film, although he himself was never known to a larger audience.

"Going out to confront the truth."

In view of the fact that Fellini tended toward neo-realism in his early screenplays and in the first films he directed, and also in light of his later rejection of neo-realism and subsequent dispute with its proponents, it would seem advisable to take a moment here to look somewhat more closely at neo-realism in the cinema.

Scene from *The Young and the Passionate* (with Jean Brochard), 1953

As we have already seen, the films shown in Mussolini's Italy were usually harmless, conciliatory entertainment which consciously avoided socially or politically sensitive subjects and which generally contained no realistic descriptions of the milieu in which the action took place. Even foreign films, insofar as they could be shown in public at all, were subject to alteration. The only world permitted in Italian dream palaces was a world purged of unpleasantness. Only as the collapse of the Fascist regime approached were Italian film-makers able to turn their attention once again to reality, and it was anything but rosy. Italian directors literally took their projects onto the streets, fired by numerous inspirations, among them recourse to Italy's own history of realistic films, new impulses from contemporary French film and the stimulus of the English documentary.

The maxim for their work was taken from Cesare Zavattini: "What I am most interested in is going out to confront the truth."[39] Making films became an examination of social reality. Films told unadorned stories of "simple" people and their problems. The harsh everday world of the wartime and post-war period made its way into the cinema, and life was shown in its actual setting. The development was introduced by such films as Vittorio De Sica's *I bambini ci guardano* (1942), the script for which was written in co-operation with Cesare Zavattini, as well as by Luchino Visconti's *Ossessione* (1942). Interestingly enough, the term neo-realism was coined in connection with *Ossessione* by Visconti's film cutter, Mario Serandrei, who dubbed the film "neo-realistic" after having seen the rushes. But *Ossessione* has not gone down in film history for this alone. A contemporary review of the film justly noted: "Faced with *Ossessione* we have to ask ourselves if we have not come to a crossroads in Italian films. Not so much because of the unusual quality of the film but because of the expressive realism that manifests itself here, perhaps for the first time in Italian film production. For what may be the first time, the protagonists speak and move in perfect harmony with their social milieu, and for the first time there was no fear of showing ugliness in order to achieve greater expressiveness."[40]

Federico Fellini, 1961

In their search for the most "authentic" expression possible, film-makers started using non-professional actors (a practice continued by Fellini later on), and instead of telling made-up stories they let life speak for itself. Zavattini, the most radical proponent of neo-realism, went so far as to demand that everything in film should be the present and that only the present should be documented there. He did not observe this limitation in his own screenplays, but that's a different story.

Neo-realism reached its high point in works by Roberto Rossellini (*Roma, città aperta*, *Paisà*, and *Germania, anno zero*). And although neo-realism lasted only a few years, it is considered one of the most important tendencies in the post-war film. It even left its mark on Hollywood.

The encounter between Fellini and Tullio Pinelli also had an influence on the history of film. Their very first meeting was the beginning of a wonderful friendship. And it was a most productive one, for Pinelli and Fellini worked closely together as scriptwriters for the next twenty years, at first for other important neo-realist directors and later on for Fellini's own pictures.

They wrote their first joint script for Alberto Lattuada's film *Senza pietà* (1947), on which Fellini also worked as assistant director. This combination of author and assistant director is to be found often in Fellini's subsequent career. Once he even took on a small part, playing the blond stranger with

Federico Fellini during filming, about 1965

Anna Magnani in Rossellini's *L'amore* (1948). This was the only time Fellini appeared in a film without playing himself.

Following his co-operation with Pietro Germi on *In nome della legge* (1948) and another film with Lattuada, *Il mulino del Po* (1949), Fellini returned to Rossellini. Together they wrote the script for *Francesco, giullare di Dio* (1950). Fellini was also assistant director for this film.

Fellini and his Work

"Why don't you make the film?"

During the same year Alberto Lattuada, with whom Fellini had worked for the first time in 1946, helped him get a job as assistant director of a special kind. (The script for Lattuada's *Il delitto di Giovanni Episcopo* was written with Tellini and two other authors at that time.) Lattuada approached Fellini with the idea of writing a script about competitors for the title of Miss Italy. Fellini had a different project in mind at the time, however, and what he really wanted to do was make a film about travelling variety theatre artists. Lattuada let himself be convinced by Fellini, and the two of them founded a company with Giulietta Masina and five other shareholders that provided a third of the money for producing *Variety Lights*. The rest of the money came from Mario Inghirami, the agent of the "Capitolium" film company.[41] The Fellini/Lattuada team of authors, who were also the film's directors, was joined by Ennio Flaiano, with whom Fellini enjoyed as deep and productive a friendship during the following years as that with Pinelli.

Variety Lights premièred in Italy in 1950. The critics responded positively to the film, but it was not very popular with the public. Fellini, who evidently had no further ambitions about becoming a director, thus returned to writing. Working in co-operation with others, he wrote the scripts for Pietro Germi's *Il cammino della Speranza* (1950), *La città si difende* (1951) and *Il brigante di tacca del Lupe* (1952). In addition Fellini worked on *Cameriera bella presenza offresi* (1951) by Giorgio Pastina and *Europa '51* by Roberto Rossellini.

Fellini had been working exclusively as a scriptwriter since 1947 and enjoyed considerable popularity; he had almost reconciled himself to the idea of earning his living this way – and he did enjoy the work: "I had it very easy as a scriptwriter: I wasn't responsible for anything because everything I wrote was reworked several times by others. When there was a good passage in a film, you could always say it was yours."[42] Fellini became a director again by chance in 1952. Fellini and Pinelli were commissioned to write a script dealing satirically with the photographic novels that were so popular in Italy at the time. Michelangelo Antonioni, whose idea it was, was foreseen as director – he had already dealt with the subject once in the short film *L'amorosa menzogna* (1949). But Antonioni didn't like the script the two friends produced under the title *The White Sheik*. "Then, while he [Antonioni] was in Bomarzo working on the documentary *La villa dei mostri*, he fell ill and Mambretti, the partner of Ponti [who was originally supposed to produce the film] convinced him to sell the idea and to give up the direction of the film in favour of Lattuada. The project wandered from one producer to another until it finally wound up with Luigi Rovere, a producer whose office was next to that of Ponti in the Lux cinema. Rovere offered the film to two or three directors. Then he thought of me. 'Actually,' he said to me, 'you did all right during the couple of days you worked on *Persiane chiuse [Closed Curtains]*...' *Persiane chiuse* was supposed to have been directed by Gianni Puccini in Turin, but then he got cold feet and Rovere sent me to encourage him. At the same time Luigi Comencini was being prepared to succeed him.

"I had directed several short scenes... but had never felt responsible, had always felt like a tourist. And after Comencini arrived, I went my own way again. But Rovère repeated his offer: 'Why don't you make the film?'... I

Fellini during an interview, about 1961

25

Fellini, about 1960

liked the idea. I had always loved adventure story comics... So one day, almost without noticing it, I had started rehearsals for *The White Sheik*. It was the first time I was a director and not just a tourist..."[43]

"A director who wants what he wants..."

A number of legends have developed around the first day of shooting for this film, but as different as the various versions are, they make one thing clear: Fellini arrived shy and helpless on the scene but left it as a self-assured director, more than that, as a "despotic director" as he calls himself. More or less overnight he became a director "who wants what he wants, demanding, petty, moody, with all of the weaknesses and characteristics that I had always hated or envied in real directors."[44]

The White Sheik premièred at the film festival in Venice in September 1952 but was not very well received. The distributor withdrew the film after just a few days. The film got a second chance only after Fellini had gained international fame with *La Strada* (1954).

One of the official reasons given for the failure of *The White Sheik* was that the star of the film, Alberto Sordi, was not popular. This sounds like a fairly weak excuse when we consider the fact that Sordi had already been the speaker for Oliver Hardy in synchronized versions of his films, that he was very popular on the radio and that he would soon be one of the most famous comedians in his country. Whatever the case may be, Fellini didn't brood over it very long. Fitted out with a more than healthy self-esteem he had already set his inner idea machine in motion again, developing a project he had been thinking about for several years one that would go down in film history as *La Strada*. But the time was not yet right for this masterpiece. No producer was willing to finance it and even Flaiano didn't like the story at first. When Fellini finally thought he had found a producer in Lorenzo Pegoraro, realization of the project was hindered by a dispute over the female lead. Fellini had written *La Strada* for his wife, but Pegoraro couldn't see Giulietta Masina in the roll of Gelsomina, not to mention the fact that he found the action too complex.

Fellini and Yvonne Fourneaux during the filming of *La Dolce Vita*, 1960

Scene from *The Young and the Passionate*, 1953

"Truth can only be stated subjectively."

In spite of their differences of opinion Pegoraro, who was an ardent admirer of Fellini, insisted on making a film with him. Fellini therefore kept an eye out for a new idea and, as was often to be the case later on, it was more or less a by-product of a social gathering that brought together the authors and friends Pinelli, Fellini, and Flaiano. This time Flaiano and Fellini supplied mutual inspiration. They started talking about memories of their youth and found that many of their experiences were similar and that they had felt many of the same things. Above all, though, it was the almost identical moments of melancholy that inspired the idea for *The Young and the Passionate (I vitelloni)* during this conversation. The film tells the story of five friends whose lives consist of doing nothing. Casting was difficult from the beginning and the fact that Fellini again wanted to work with Alberto Sordi made the producer Pegoraro especially unhappy. What made matters even worse was that Fellini's list of actors contained not a single star. Pegoraro, who didn't want to run the risk of financing a failure, asked Fellini to get in touch with the famous actor and director Vittorio de Sica to see if he couldn't get him to co-operate on the film. Fellini went to see de Sica and offered him a role. De Sica didn't seem to be disinclined toward acting in Fellini's new film but the desired engagement never came off – something Fellini wasn't all too sorry about, although he would like to have worked once with de Sica.

After the completion of *The Young and the Passionate* in the spring of 1953, the old claim that Alberto Sordi's name had a negative effect on the box office was resurrected. It was thus removed from the posters and from the first copies of the film without any harm to his popularity. *The Young and the Passionate* represented Sordi's well-deserved film breakthrough. After this co-operative effort with Fellini he became one of the busiest actors in Italy.

The première of *The Young and the Passionate* at the Biennale in Venice was awaited with great interest. But that was still six months away, and Fellini used the time to make the short film *Un' agenzia matrimoniale (The Marriage*

Broker) with drama students at the Centro Sperimentale di Cinematografia. This work was part of the episodic film *Love in the City* which, like so many other episodic films of this time, went back to an idea by Cesare Zavattini. *Love in the City* appeared in cinemas in 1953 but did not enjoy much popularity, although Fellini's episode was well received.

Fellini was more successful with *The Young and the Passionate*, which premièred exactly one year later in Venice. As the American director Peter Bogdanovich said, "These two films alone would have made Fellini one of the great directors"[45].

Giulietta Masina as Gelsomina in *La Strada*, 1954

The audience and the critics were not ready to pass such positive judgment at the time, but *The Young and the Passionate* was nevertheless so successful that it was the first of Fellini's films to be picked up by international distributors. It subsequently inspired directors all over the world who were interested in such themes.[46]

The former caricaturist and scriptwriter had now aroused interest outside his own country, and the brochure *Der Film in Europa* (1955) says: "The most surprising thing about contemporary Italian film is how often talented scriptwriters turn to directing. One name stands out above all the others: Federico Fellini, who formerly collaborated with Rossellini and who gave us an apt portrayal of Italian youth – or rather of a group of young unemployed Italians in the countryside – in the film *The Young and the Passionate* in 1953."[47]

In spite of the realistic study of the milieu depicted in *The Young and the Passionate*, leftist film critics, who formed the main body of support for neo-realism, began to dissociate themselves from Fellini: "Even though there was a good deal of approval, I was charged with having set the film in a provincial milieu that lacked exact social coordinates. I was accused of being all too caught up in the poetry of memory and of not having given the film a clear political direction."[48] Fellini probably didn't have the latter in mind at all. On the contrary – he was in the middle of a phase during which he was developing his own personal film world of dreams, memories and visions. The external image of reality supplied only the background, played at most a symbolic role in his concept of film. For Fellini, the neo-realist dogma of the representation of social reality made less and less sense. He was increasingly interested in psychological reality, the poetry of introspection, drawing on his own inner life as most immediately accessible. The break with neo-realism was therefore inevitable and finally came with *La Strada*, Fellini's next film.

But first he had to find a producer. In 1954, after a good deal of effort, he found two – Carlo Ponti and Dino de Laurentiis – who were willing to finance the film story of the circus couple Gelsomina and Zampano.

La Strada is, of course, more than just the story of an ill-matched couple. It is a parable about isolation and as such it completely rejects any neo-realist claim to being a portrayal of reality, even if the film is supposed to be based on actual events. If we can believe Fellini, the idea for *La Strada* grew out of Fellini's chance encounter with a gypsy couple, a kind of human still-life that would busy his imagination for some time: the image was of a couple sitting at the edge of the road eating. To Fellini, the two looked as if they "led only a physical existence and as if there was no longer any emotional contact between them."[49]

Fellini's deeply moving experience of human isolation was then incorporated into a film story set among street entertainers. There is no question but that Fellini saw his wife, Giulietta Masina, in the leading female role from the beginning. Masina herself has said: "Gelsomina grew like a child during the more than ten years of our marriage as my husband watched and observed me. He drew the figure again and again in his sketchbooks and was inspired to give it final form by many details, especially the facial expression he discovered in photographs of me as a child, in particular my habit of smiling with closed lips. This certain smile became one of the characteristic expressions of the film figure Gelsomina."[50]

Like Pegoraro before them, the producers Ponti and de Laurentiis were not convinced about Masina at the beginning. De Laurentiis, for example, saw Silvana Mangano in the role of Gelsomina and Burt Lancaster as her partner. Again, and not for the last time, Fellini had to fight to realize his aims regarding casting.

It is actually quite surprising that no one had recognized Fellini's talent for casting up to this point. Instead of signing up stars who would guarantee big profits at the box office, Fellini insisted even then on peopling his film world with the faces that seemed right to him. He had always had an idea of certain types of people for his stories, and a famous actor or actress only got a role if he or she corresponded to Fellini's idea of the figure to be played. Although this frequently led to disputes with his financial backers, the results always showed that Fellini was right. But producers never felt completely comfortable with Fellini's approach. This was the case with *La Strada* too, and Fellini had to use all his arts of persuasion to win them over to his desired team of Giulietta Masina and Anthony Quinn.

La Strada premièred at the Venice film festival on September 6, 1954, to a frosty reception by the audience.[51] However, after it had begun its regular run in cinemas, it was received enthusiastically by audiences all over the world. The French director André Cayatte, for instance, says that Fellini's film was "a classic" from the beginning.[52] *La Strada* received the Silver Lion at the festival, but this was just the beginning of a flood of national and international prizes, 148 altogether, among them an Oscar for Best Foreign Film.

La Strada was also an enormous success at the box office, bringing in twenty times the investment made in its production. It also brought Fellini's wife world-wide fame. It is not surprising that Fellini was asked to make a sequel, but he refused, just as he had already refused to do a sequel to *The Young and the Passionate*. Nor did he accept Walt Disney's idea of making an animated film about Gelsomina,[53] even though the cartoon medium points to the origins of at least the name if not the figure of Gelsomina herself: Gelsomina is the feminine version of Gelsomino, the name of a horse in the comic book series *Fortunello* which Fellini had always enjoyed reading.

The story of Gelsomina thus had no sequel in films, but the *La Strada* cult was exploited commercially in many other ways, for example in Gelsomina dolls, cigars called "Zampano" and pubs and restaurants all over the world that called and still call themselves "La Strada". In this context, it is also interesting to take note of the career of the music for the film composed by Nino Rota. It formed the basis for the hit "Stars Shine in Your Eyes" in the United States[54] and in Italy it was arranged for a ballet which was also called "La Strada" and which premièred at La Scala.[55]

All this commotion about a film comes as a surprise to no one nowadays, but it should be remembered that what seem like normal marketing strategies in the film industry today were the exception at the time. Even by today's standards, however, the plans of a small Dutch village, Nierberg, would be unique: The town's notables offered Fellini a lifetime position as mayor.[56] (If Fellini had accepted the offer, he would have been decades ahead of his American colleague Clint Eastwood, who became mayor of his hometown, Carmel, in 1986.)

In the meantime, neo-realists and leftist film critics created a different kind of commotion over Fellini and his work. They, and above all Zavattini, charged Fellini with having betrayed the basic principles of neo-realism. His own personal view of the world had distorted reality in *La Strada* and it was thus to be condemned. Fellini, who couldn't quite understand the reason for the criticism, answered his adversaries in an open letter in which he said: "Sometimes a film that embodies the conflicting feelings of a period in an

Giulietta Masina and Anthony Quinn in *La Strada*, 1954

Scene from *La Strada* with Richard Basehart as Matto and Giulietta Masina, 1954

Anthony Quinn as Zampanò and Giulietta
Masina in *La Strada*, 1954

elementary dialectic, in more or less mythic figures, is far more realistic than
one that takes as its point of reference a developing socio-political reality.
That's why I don't believe in 'objectivity', at least not in objectivity as you
understand it. That's why I cannot share your view of neo-realism, which not
only does not exhaust but does not even suggest the possibilities of the
movement with which I have identified myself since *Roma, città aperta*."[57]

The principle of "objectivity" to which the neo-realists attached such
dogmatic importance had always been only a tentative guideline for Fellini's
work. His definition of neo-realism went far beyond the one laid down by his
colleagues: "To me neo-realism is a kind of unprejudiced vision, fully free of
the pressure of conventions, in short a willingness to confront reality without
preconceived notions... It is a question of developing a feel for reality,
although an interpretation is, of course, always necessary. For why should
people go to the cinema if films only show them perceived reality from a cold
and objective perspective? In this case it would be better to go out into the
streets. To me neo-realism means observing reality, every kind of reality,
from an honest perspective: not only social reality, but intellectual, metaphy-
sical reality, everything that is in man... To me neo-realism does not express
itself in what we show but in how we show it."[58]

Naturally enough, Fellini was able to convince the neo-realist dogmatists
with the broad interpretations in which he claims for himself and his work a
"personal realism"[59], especially since an idea that was later to cause problems
for others also shines through here: Fellini's highly individual concept of

reality and truth. His frequently cited claim that he is a liar but an honest one says it all. And if we see this claim in connection with his comment that the truth can only be expressed subjectively[60], then we begin to understand somewhat better his personal sense of ethics and to a certain extent therefore also his understanding of his own art.

Even after neo-realism had passed Fellini was often charged with distorting reality. Fellini just as frequently answered that he was simply representing reality anew – not changing it, but reconstructing it as he saw it. And besides, he said, he had little sympathy for cinematic truth: "I am more in favour of the cinematic lie. A lie is always more interesting than the truth. The lie is the soul of acting, and I love theatre... The things you show don't have to be believable. Generally it is better if they are not. What has to be believable is the emotion that is felt in the expression and in the viewing."[61]

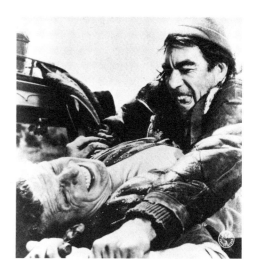

Scene from *La Strada*, 1954, with Anthony Quinn (right) and Richard Basehart (left)

In 1970 Fellini formulated the following hypothesis in accordance with the results of perception research in the social sciences and in keeping with philosophic thought on the problem of cognitive activity[62]: "We cannot judge reality without adopting a point of view. If you watch the news on television, you will see how strange everything looks. That's the way it is. Without comment! Without us! There simply is no reality without us – and I don't mean me but all of us!"[63] And, he added polemically, "Reality distorts!"

But Fellini's tendency toward a particularly subjective view of reality is certainly not merely the result of his own love of polemics. In her noteworthy book on Fellini, Liliana Betti, his collaborator and friend of many years, gives us a few useful hints in this regard: "Is Fellini just a common liar with all of the pathological qualities this implies, or is he an individual who is eaten up by his innate weakness for fantasy, driven to expand, distort and form anew the facts and experience of reality? Without a doubt, he belongs to the second category by nature – and to the first because he pursues this nature so consistently."[64]

Fellini not only pursues this natural bent consistently, he has turned it into a view of life that inevitably influences his work. He is a realist in the service of the imagination, one who is attracted by everything that stimulates the fantasy. The fact that he has a special relationship with the irrational has already been mentioned. It can come as no surprise, therefore, that Fellini is especially attracted by magic and by madness – in its most literal sense. His frequent visits to psychiatric clinics have provided him with many ideas for his films, for instance *The Clowns* (1970), in which the Brothers Fratellini make an appearance in an asylum. At one time Fellini even wanted to make a film that had been written by the director of such a clinic: "I spent three months in his clinic dressed as a doctor. But when I left the clinic I couldn't make the film. I sensed the danger. It is very difficult to remain on this side of the border when you have once come so close to it...."[65]

Another project that Fellini never completed, although parts of it were used for *Roma*, was "Moraldo in città". It was thought of as a continuation of the story of one of the five loafers in *The Young and the Passionate*. The treatment was published in the Italian film magazine *Cinema*.[66] The film was to have been made after *La Strada* in 1955, but plans were shelved for the time being after Fellini had an idea for another project during work on *La Strada*. The idea for the film *The Swindle (Il Bidone)* came from an encounter with a stranger who told Fellini his life story. Of particular interest to Fellini was the way the man earned his living, travelling from village to village selling cheap fabric at high prices. This kind of con game must have amused Fellini, given his own tendency toward distorting the facts, and he decided to make a film set in such a milieu. Initially Fellini conceived of the story in more or less picturesque and harmless terms, but the deeper he and his collaborators delved into the world of Roman fraud, the more serious they realized the

Broderick Crawford (left) as Augusto and
Richard Basehart as Picasso in *The Swindle*,
1955

subject was. The conversations he carried on with small-time swindlers made
it clear that he was dealing with a hard and cruel reality. It now seemed
inappropriate to him to use the material for a comedy and he decided to make
a film which was based on authentic figures. The screenplay, which was
written in co-operation with Flaiano and Pinelli, concentrated on the story of
one swindler, drawing to a large extent on statements made by the underworld figures the writers had interviewed. The title of the film, *Il bidone*,
comes from the language of the Roman underworld and means "cheater" as
well as "cheating". Fellini originally wanted the lead to be played by Hum-
phrey Bogart but finally decided on Broderick Crawford. The decision was a
wise but unhappy one, wise because Crawford gives a devastating portrayal
of the swindler Augusto, but unhappy because Crawford was an alcoholic at
the time and his drunkenness complicated work on the film.[67]

The Swindle was first shown at the Biennale in Venice on September 8,
1955, but both the audience and the critics reacted coolly. They had expected
a comedy; what they got was a tragedy. There were no really damning
reviews, but Fellini was charged with having told a drawn-out and confused
story.[68] Fellini revised the film, but the new version, which was thirty minutes
shorter, was no better received than the first. *The Swindle* disappeared from
the cinema and was only rediscovered several years later. It is now regarded as
one of Fellini's most important early works.

The initial failure of *The Swindle* made Fellini more cautious about the
choice of material for his films. It wasn't that he dissociated himself from his
previous works or that he moved toward films that promised more commercial success – Federico Fellini never made concessions of that kind. But
failures have always been a bad calling card in the film business. Possible

projects were scrutinized even more closely, but none of them were right. And then Fellini remembered a story that he had been mulling over, like *La Strada*, for some time, indeed since his co-operation with Roberto Rossellini on *L'amore* in 1947. At that time Fellini had suggested making a film about a Roman prostitute. He envisioned Anna Magnani in the lead – but she turned out to be anything but enthusiastic about the idea. (Fifteen years were to pass before Magnani overcame her reservations about playing a prostitute and took on such a role in *Mamma Roma* (1962), but then it was for Pier Paolo Pasolini.)

Magnani's rejection of the role killed the idea for Rossellini, but the project remained alive in Fellini's mind. He continued to reflect on the unrealized project and to collect material for the plot, even during the filming of *The Swindle*, during which he met the prostitute Wanda in one of the seedier areas of Rome. Wanda's confessions and the circumstances of her life helped form Fellini's ideas but the film got its name and face from a figure who had appeared briefly in his first feature film, *The White Sheik*. Then, too, the figure of the prostitute Cabiria had been played by Giulietta Masina; in his new film, *The Nights of Cabiria*, the action was to center around this same figure. After a long search for financial backing Dino de Laurentiis agreed to produce the film, but preparations were overshadowed by the sudden death of Fellini's father, who suffered a heart attack on May 31, 1956.

Scene from *The Swindle*, 1955

"Gelsomina's fallen sister."

In retrospect it is fortunate that Anna Magnani turned down the role of the prostitute at the time, for Cabiria shouldn't have been played by anyone but

Richard Basehart, Giulietta Masina and Federico Fellini during filming of *The Swindle*, 1955

Giulietta Masina – nothing against the great Magnani! Masina's short appearance in *The White Sheik* had proven the point, and Fellini must have known it as well. Like the role of Gelsomina, that of Cabiria was tailor-made for his wife. As far as the appearance of the two figures was concerned, Fellini emphasized Masina's clown-like nature in both of them, especially her expressive talent for mimicry. Giulietta Masina has an inimitable ability to depict figures who are laughing on one side and crying on the other, with the moody inner life of the figure mirrored in her face. If she cries, laughter chases sadness from her eyes a moment later. Watching her means experiencing a constant change in feeling and mood.

Fellini made use of all these possibilities and it is certainly not a matter of mere chance that Cabiria resembles Gelsomina in so many ways. Masina's portrayal seems to establish a relationship between them. Justifiably enough, Cabiria has often been called "Gelsomina's fallen sister", though the fact that Cabiria is a streetwalker is only partially symbolic: "I chose a prostitute as the main figure both because of my preference for extremes and because, objectively seen, the relations between a man and a prostitute are among the most brutal there are."[69]

If Fellini hadn't repeatedly maintained that he had never seen early film masterpieces, that he almost never went to the movies, we could assume that the name "Cabiria" is a kind of homage to the monumental *Cabiria* of 1914, directed by Giovanni Pastrone. The assumption would be a natural one insofar as Pastrone was the first director, in *Cabiria*, to make use of techniques that have since become accepted film-making practice and were always part of Fellini's own basic approach. Pastrone's innovations included the use of artificial light, the use of a mobile camera and the construction of realistic sets (up to then the background, e.g. buildings, had just been painted).[70] Even if Fellini never did hear anything about Pastrone's contributions to film-making, he would surely have been fascinated by his innovations with regard to scenery, for the reconstruction of reality in seemingly realistic studio sets has always appealed to Fellini.

In order to be able to draw a realistic portrait of Cabiria's milieu, Fellini and his co-authors visited the areas they wanted to describe. Pier Paolo Pasolini,

Broderick Crawford in *The Swindle*, 1955

whom Fellini had met by chance and with whom he quickly became friends,
turned out to be of great help. He introduced Fellini to the dark side of Rome,
the Rome of excess, nightly revels and idleness. This atmosphere was also to
provide Fellini with the inspiration for his next film, *La Dolce Vita*.

Pasolini's co-operation on *The Nights of Cabiria* was not limited to his role
as guide to the city; he also worked actively on the screenplay and was
responsible for the dialogues in the original Roman dialect. This is one of the
nuances that is lost in the process of synchronization; in the dubbed version
there is no dialect of any kind to be heard.

The première of *The Nights of Cabiria* took place at the Cannes film festival
in March 1957. The film was an enormous success from the beginning and the
triumph included Giulietta Masina, who was named best actress at the festival. In the United States, where Fellini's films have been very popular, *The
Nights of Cabiria* won the Oscar for Best Foreign Film, the New York
Critics' award and ten years later received a special acknowledgement in the
form of a musical based on the story of Cabiria. On Broadway Cabiria was
called "Sweet Charity", and *Sweet Charity* was in turn filmed, with Shirley
MacLaine in the title role, by Bob Fosse.

But Fellini's new work won recognition and prizes not only abroad. The
applause came from Italian film audiences as well and new awards filled his
house, although the Catholic Church and circles close to it expressed such
great reservations about the film that it seemed for a while it might be

Giulietta Masina as Cabiria in *The Nights of Cabiria*, 1957

forbidden. The reason for the protest, apart from the questionable subject of the film, was the fact that innocence and purity were embodied by, of all people, a prostitute. Nevertheless the International Catholic Film Office listed *The Nights of Cabiria* as an exemplary film "because it reveals human selfishness and counters this with the virtues of justice and Christian charity."[71] But the film is exemplary in another way as well, for here Fellini, the master of cinematographic sensuousness, portrays his protagonist Cabiria as one of the most asexual prostitutes in film history.

"A documentary film about life."

While Fellini's story of the fate of a streetwalker had caused differences of opinion among Catholics, his next film was to lead to a hardening of the lines of conflict. There was no more praise from the Catholic Church although the Holy See had approved the script and had even given permission for Fellini to film in St. Peter's in Rome.

Even more persistently than in the case of *The Nights of Cabiria* the Vatican insisted that *La Dolce Vita* should be removed from cinemas. The film was repeatedly attacked from the pulpit and people were advised not to go and see it. But it wasn't enough that the film was a bone of contention to the Church; the Italian parliament also took up the subject at the insistence of some of its members and senators – a fate that may be unique in the history of moving pictures. The parliament actually did debate the question of prohibiting *La Dolce Vita* but the government fortunately refused to censor the film and spoke out in general against such censorship. What was it that led to this Church and State affair, the effects of which were felt in Argentina, where *La Dolce Vita* could only be shown in bowdlerized form?

During his research for *The Nights of Cabiria*, Fellini's attention had been drawn to a phenomenon that documented the decay of Italian social structures in particularly typical fashion: people in certain circles in Rome were leading a life of dissolution and wild extravagance, making no secret of their weariness of life. Fellini, who had always been interested in the negative side of human existence, could not forget what he had seen. After completion of *The Nights of Cabiria* he plunged once more into the milieu of the idle rich, whose one interest seemed to be in living as luxurious and sweet a life as possible. Fellini saw the Via Veneto in Rome as the centre of this life of pleasure. He stayed there for several months, observing the antics of the aristocracy, of the arrogant *nouveaux riches,* the affected Bohemians, the decadent intellectuals. Fellini was once again on the trail of clues, one of his favourite activities. He wanted to wring from life details that could be used for film. The creative power of his cinematographic vision drew its energy once more from the external world. But Fellini was not the only one who had chosen the cafés and bars of the Via Veneto as a post from which to make his observations. Numerous photographers working for the popular press were doing research on stories about Roman High Society on location. And true to the stereotype of a certain kind of journalist, if there wasn't a story to be had, then the facts were simply touched up a little.[72] In time Fellini became acquainted with some of the press photographers, which really wasn't very difficult for him. In chatting with them he learned a good deal more about the Via Veneto and the smart set that pursued its pleasures there. But Fellini also noted his conversation partners most closely, and they were incorporated into his film as caricatures later on.

The screenplay, written in collaboration with Flaiano and Pinelli, was completed in autumn 1958 and incorporated events that had drawn a great deal of attention in the popular press all over the world that year.[73] The impressions Fellini had gathered during his research for the film also found

Scene from *The Nights of Cabiria,* 1957

François Périer and Giulietta Masina in *The Nights of Cabiria,* 1957

their atmospheric expression here, as did several scenes that were highly provocative for the times. All in all, Fellini's chronicle of scandal created a scandal itself. But first Fellini had to find a producer for the project, no easy task since it was expected "in film circles that the film would be a flop from the beginning", as Fellini himself remembers.[74]

After the problem of financing had been solved by signing a contract with Riama Film (Alberto Rizzoli and Giuseppe Amato), Fellini commissioned Piero Gherardi to begin work on the sets and costumes. (Gherardi, who had already done the sets for *The Nights of Cabiria*, would also create an effective atmosphere for Fellini's next films.)

After *La Dolce Vita* stage design began to take on ever greater importance for Fellini, not only because the films that followed were created for the most part in the studio. Costumes, props and stage design are, along with the sets, an expression of the reality being portrayed, but they also call up an atmosphere that is necessary for the representation of Fellini's inner reality – his dreams, his longings, his memories, visions and fears. Part of Fellini's inner life is visualized in the sets and stage designs and this creates a strong emotional bond between the director and the art director, set designer and property man. The degree of mutual influence is unusually great and Fellini, who never let other people influence his work, always listens willingly to their suggestions. It is not unusual for Fellini to be inspired to create completely new scenes by such co-operation. The tyrant grants his master builders an audience! But Fellini also expected an extraordinary performance from these members of his team. For *La Dolce Vita* this meant that Gherardi and his colleagues had to recreate a substantial part of the Via Veneto in Studio 14 of Cinecittà because of the difficulties involved in working on location. Shooting was also delayed by the fact that Fellini still didn't know who it was he wanted for certain roles. Only the lead actor had been decided upon fairly early. The gossip columnist Marcello Rubini who chronicles the events in the film was to be played by the still unknown Marcello Mastroianni. Fellini had succeeded in getting his way here, in spite of the pressure put on him by producers who would like to have seen an international star in the role. Given the success of the film Mastroianni was to become their international star after the fact. But Mastroianni was not the only one who was showered with recognition – it also went to his film partner Anita Ekberg and, of course, to Fellini, for whom *La Dolce Vita* represented a breakthrough to national and international recognition as a director.

This all lay ahead of him, though, and Fellini first had to complete the cast. Silvana Mangano, Barbara Stanwyck, Henry Fonda and Peter Ustinov were among those seriously considered but not signed in the long run. The search for a suitable cast repeatedly provided the popular press with headlines and ended only after a period of several months. The result was that many members of Roman high society played themselves in *La Dolce Vita*.

Shooting lasted six months and produced 92,000 metres of film[75] – enough for nearly 56 hours of screening.

Fellini worked on the material for three months and in the end the finished version was almost three hours long, the first Italian film of such exceptional length.[76] Even now, a film this long is an exception, and although many of Fellini's later films were more than two hours long, none of them were as long as *La Dolce Vita* – though quantity says nothing, of course, about quality.

La Dolce Vita got its start in a number of private showings in February 1960 and it became clear relatively early on that the film would have a tremendous impact. During the première in Milan, for example, the film was booed and Fellini, who was in attendance, was spat on by people in the audience who felt their national honour had been sullied. With his depiction of high living

Marcello Mastroianni and Anita Ekberg in *La Dolce Vita*, 1960

Marcello Mastroianni as a scandal reporter in *La Dolce Vita*, 1960

among the Roman smart set Fellini was thought to have dragged all of Italy through the mud. The most common charge made against him and his film was that they were "amoral".

But *La Dolce Vita*, which Fellini considers "a documentary film about life"[77], was also accorded a great deal of recognition, especially by those who saw it as a critical portrait of society. The Soviet ambassador in Rome was evidently among this part of Fellini's audience, thanking Fellini for the portrayal of the bourgeois decline of morals with a comradely kiss on the cheek. Today we can only smile at many of the passages in the film that were damned as amoral at the time, and the fundamental statement of *La Dolce Vita* remains valid. It may in fact be even more valid now than it was then, given the increasing isolation of the individual and the growing feeling of the senselessness of life among many people.

In any case, the scandal the film caused naturally created a great deal of publicity, which in the long run turned the film into one of Fellini's most popular works. Its commercial success was then crowned by "half the larger and smaller prizes that are awarded on this planet" – as Tullio Kezich put it.[78] This included among others the top award at the film festival in Cannes in 1960 and an Oscar for the black and white costumes in 1961. It also received Oscar nominations for best screenplay, best direction and best production.

"Producers always want to change the ending."

La Dolce Vita represented Fellini's final break with the traditional narrative approach to film-making. His films had rarely had a smooth-flowing plot in any case. In accordance with the aesthetics of neo-realism his stories were often made up of a series of episodes, and this approach not only gave *La Dolce Vita* its character but later became a trademark of Fellini's work.

Fellini was not only in the process of revolutionizing cinematic style, he was also providing decisive new impulses for the subject matter treated in film. Whereas Italian films of the post-war years had been dominated by neo-realism, drawing on everyday social occurrences for their themes, Fellini

Scene from *La Dolce Vita*, 1960

Scene from *La Dolce Vita* with Anita Ekberg, 1960

began to turn increasingly to the portrayal of inner life, away from society and towards the individual with his complex world of feelings and dreams. Along with directors such as Michelangelo Antonioni, though working independently, Fellini began to concentrate on the psychological aspects of experience in the 60's. In fact he came to play a central role in the development of what specialists later called the "psychological film"[79]. Fellini's turn toward the emotional life of his figures was probably the result of his friendship with the psychologist Ernst Bernhard – a pupil of Carl Gustav Jung – who introduced Fellini to the ideas of his teacher. Fellini listened to Jung's theories with fascination and found in them a source of creative ideas. They were to bear fruit for the first time in *Juliet of the Spirits (Giulietta degli spiriti)*.

First, though, Fellini turned his efforts towards a project that was never realized. In order to give himself and also younger but as yet unknown filmmakers a chance to establish a type of film that deviated ever more from the established norm, Fellini and Angelo Rizzoli – who had raised the money for *La Dolce Vita* – co-founded their own production and distributing company, FEDERIZ, in 1961. Fellini wrote about his plans at the time in *Films and filming*: "I want to surround myself with seafarers, storytellers and jesters, as in a medieval court. But there will be no despotism. I know what it means for a young director to fight against the despotism of producers. Maybe I survived myself because I created a protective wall around me. For others it is not so easy. They don't all have my fanaticism and they let themselves be browbeaten. If I had to give a definition of the policy of my company, I would say that it is one that will never make its directors change the endings of their films. Producers always want to change the endings. I shall leave the director to do as he wishes. Rizzoli has had faith in me. I shall have faith in my directors."[80]

Fellini began his new task full of enthusiasm and, as Pier Paolo Pasolini – one of the first to be supported by FEDERIZ – said, "as happily and as proudly as a child, and of course a little coyly."[81] But Fellini tired of the undertaking quickly. And FEDERIZ went bankrupt after just a short time, without ever having really produced a film. The fact that the company appeared in the credits of *Juliet of the Spirits* four years later is to be understood mainly as a gesture of homage. Fellini himself sees this failure from its positive side for after all, as he says, he did "have a good time"[82].

During the period when he was supporting the next generation of film-makers Fellini continued to pursue his own film projects. Only one of them was realized, however, and then only as part of an episodic film inspired by – who else – Cesare Zavattini. The film was called *Boccaccio '70* and the episode contributed by Fellini was *The Temptation of Doctor Antonio (Le tentazioni del Dottor Antonio)*. This amusing short film, in which Fellini evidently satirized the moralists who had attacked him for *La Dolce Vita*, was Fellini's first film in colour. Every one of his previous films had been done in black and white.

Searching for new forms of expression, Fellini simply wanted to see if colour would add anything to his work. He doesn't seem to have been particularly convinced by the results, for in his next film he returned to his favourite black and white medium. In the long run, however, Fellini could not resist the pull of colour. In a reversal of Samuel Fuller's statement that life takes place in colour but black and white is more realistic,[83] Fellini found that he needed colour in order to portray more realistically his vision of a dream-like life.

The use of colour created problems for him, though, as he found out while making *Juliet of the Spirits*: "I had to try to co-ordinate two things that are contrary by nature: colour and film. I found out that colour is a static, unmoving form, whereas the nature of film is movement and constant change. If you look at a painting, you see that it changes according to the way the light falls on it. That's why the decision about where to hang a picture is almost as important as the choice of the picture itself. I think that's also the reason why artists are usually touchy on the subject of museum directors. In making a film, my camera is moving all the time. As we were getting ready to shoot, we filmed the players against different static, coloured backgrounds, and I could see even in the first footage that these surfaces never remained the same. When the light fell on them from one direction they had a certain emotional expressiveness, but when it came from another direction, or if the intensity and the quality of the light changed, then there was suddenly a completely different background. Of course this changed the entire atmosphere of a take.

Anouk Aimée as Maddalena in *La Dolce Vita*, 1960

Federico Fellini and Anita Ekberg during filming of *The Temptation of Dr. Antonio*, 1961

The actors' make-up, even the meaning of their expressions, was given a
different value by the changing surroundings. I had to plan very carefully. I
had to predict and take into my calculations the changes in the expressive
value of colour given the movements of the camera and of objects. I had to
take all of this into account; if I wanted to achieve a certain colour effect, I had
to arrange for the changes that could result from a certain situation. The set
designer had to go back a step further and construct scenery that would
produce the desired effect given the conditions of the lighting and camera
movement we had decided on. It was all very complicated."[84]

The shooting of *The Temptation of Doctor Antonio* must have been just as
complicated since Fellini was not only working with colour but also with
what was for him an unusually large number of special effects. These effects
were necessary in order to portray the inner struggle of the apostle of
morality, Antonio.

The Temptation of Doctor Antonio marks the beginning of Fellini's continuing journey into the inner life of his protagonists, although "protagonist"
doesn't always mean a film figure in the literal sense. Fellini is not only
interested in the individual's inner world but in the soul of all seemingly
closed systems, as well. It is hardly surprising, therefore, that he investigated
the psyche of his hometown by choice in *Roma* (1972) and the nature of his
professional milieu, Cinecittà, in *Intervista* (1987).

Fellini's first films were concerned with the actual world and the stories
were set in real places. The focus of the events was always the external world,
in relation to which Fellini's figures were outsiders. After his turn to the inner
world, to the soul of man, or rather after his turn to the "subconscious of

Anita Ekberg in *The Temptation of Dr. Antonio*, 1961

closed systems", it was natural to try to reconstruct these systems in the isolation of closed space. Fellini retreated ever further into the isolation of the film studio. The studio, where he was free to be a "demiurge", as he likes to call himself, became a symbol for a closed inner world. Here he could create, with absolute consistency, the type of film he had always propagated, one based on the "realism of the personal realm".

In this sense, one of his most personal films was the one that followed *Boccaccio '70* (which appeared in cinemas in February 1962 without great success)–*8 1/2*. At first this was only the working title for an expressly "comic film" derived from the number of feature films Fellini had made to date. The sum only comes out right, though, if you know that Fellini counted his short films (*Un'agenzia matrimoniale* and *The Temptation of Doctor Antonio*) as well as the film with which he made his debut, *Variety Lights* (with Alberto Lattuada), as half a film each.

"La masturbation d'un genie."

If we look more carefully at the way *8 1/2* came into existence, we can't help but get the impression that the film, like its title, was the result of a makeshift arrangement. It began with an idea Fellini had while he was staying at Chiancciano for his health. He wanted to make a film "in which the past, the present and the imaginary overlap."[85] He wanted "to pick out a certain point in a person's life, a day, an hour, actually only one moment, and then show how this moment is experienced on three different levels. A man was supposed to go to a health resort for a cure."[86]

This was the rather vague starting point for the film but, since Fellini was in good standing with his producers following the commercial success of *La Dolce Vita*, the idea provided enough of a basis for a signed contract. He was given a free hand–for a film whose production was eventually going to cost more than two million pounds. At the time the figure was unusually high.

Even during preparations for shooting it became clear that Fellini didn't really know what kind of a film he was making. More seriously, he sensed that his inspiration was fading. It went so far that the date for actual filming was repeatedly postponed and Fellini finally wanted to give up the whole project. It is no exaggeration to say that his helplessness and confusion were the result of psychoanalysis, which he had started a year before and which he broke off just before he began work on *8 1/2*.

The fact that Fellini changed his mind about psychoanalysis did not mean that he turned his back on psychology. The subject continued to interest him and he was still particularly interested in the ideas of the psychologist Carl Gustav Jung. During his first discussions with Jung's pupil Ernst Bernhard, Fellini had become a great admirer of the psychologist because he felt that Jung "had found a point of contact between science and magic, rationality and the imagination."[87] A reading of Jung's works opened Fellini's eyes in many ways. For one thing, he owed his critical stance toward the Catholic Church to Jungian psychotherapy.[88] But Jung was also a source of constant inspiration for Fellini's work.

Fellini's fascination with Jung was probably a result of the fact that, in contrast to Jung's famous colleague Sigmund Freud, the Swiss psychologist tried to explain human behaviour from the point of view of its philosophical as well as religious and mystical aspects. Jung's theory of personality is especially interesting in this regard.[89] Fellini gave this theory cinematic expression in *8 1/2* as well as in the following film, *Juliet of the Spirits*, and later, though from a different perspective, in *Fellini Satyricon*. It was no accident that *8 1/2* was originally supposed to be released with the title "Asanisimasa",

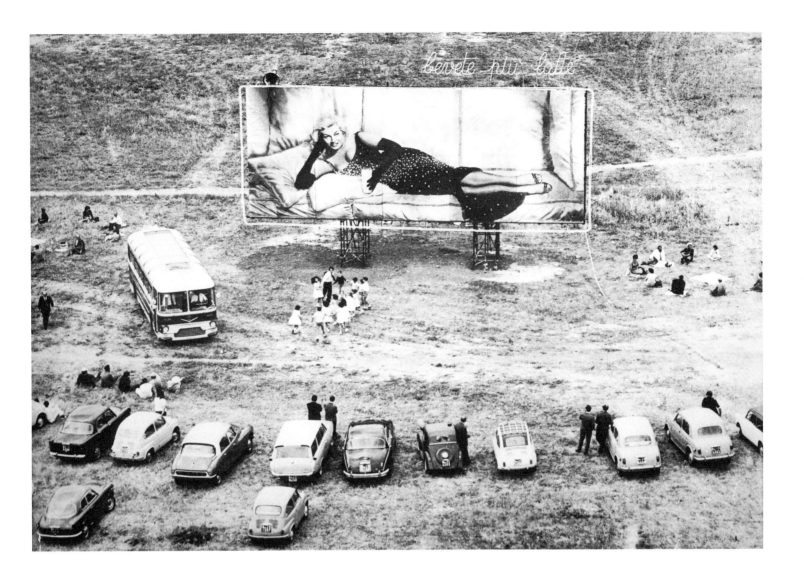

Scene from *The Temptation of Dr. Antonio*, 1961

a newly coined term in which, tellingly enough, the word anima or "soul" is embedded. In addition, Fellini spoke of *8 1/2* as a "difficult to define thing somewhere between a disjointed psychoanalytical session and a somewhat haphazard examination of conscience in an obscure atmosphere."[90] In any case, the film "did him a lot of good", especially since dealing with the subject of the creative crisis of a director helped him to escape his own seemingly hopeless situation.

The honesty with which Fellini presented himself to his public in *8 1/2*, providing them with "testimony of his inner insecurity", is remarkable.[92] And so was his decision, following the commotion in the media that accompanied the making of *La Dolce Vita*, to bar the public from the making of his new film. Regarded by many as a simple advertising gimmick, it resulted quite naturally from the fact that Fellini himself still didn't know where the film would lead: "For me *8 1/2* is a journey with an unknown destination. I change the screenplay with each day's work and I'll change many more things during editing."[93] There were even two different versions of the ending. Deena Boyer, who was responsible for press relations during the making of *8 1/2*, spoke in this context of an "end that just won't end"[94]. For a whole month the film crew was told repeatedly that filming would be completed within a few days.

Under these conditions even Fellini himself couldn't explain the roles and the plot to the actors and actresses working on the film. But what can be explained here as the result of his own ignorance about how the story would end was to become part of Fellini's normal working procedure in the future. After *8 1/2*, to avoid having actors and actresses interpret their roles and involve him in discussions about how the figures should be portrayed, Fellini simply stopped giving them the complete screenplay. He revealed to them only as much as was necessary for shooting the next day, sometimes, annoyingly enough, not even that much.

The general lack of information about what was going on behind the tightly guarded doors of the studios at Cinecittà and what was meant by the vague title *8 1/2* set the press rumour mills in motion. The craziest and most absurd conjectures about Fellini's new film found their way into print. One report said for instance that *8 1/2* was about "an expedition into space by circus artists (with elephants!), avant-garde theatre people and cocktail waitresses, who don't know themselves what they're looking for."[95] Fellini was greatly amused by these stories and, in answer to assertions that *8 1/2* was a film version of his own life story, he often gladly said: "Even if it were a film about a flounder, it would be about me in the long run."[96]

This was clear enough. Basically, it was too clear for Fellini, for it does bear witness to the identification of an artist with his work. In admitting this, he had to admit to himself that it is his soul that breathes from the screen, laid bare before an unknown audience. It is understandable that he had misgivings about this film. Fellini has often acknowledged that his films are autobiographical, but his admission is frequently followed by a partial denial: No, no, they're not all that autobiographical, after all, almost everything has been invented and he hopes that the film concerns everyone. But this is sometimes a vain hope, given the subjective nature of the films Fellini makes. After the première of *8 1/2* in February 1963, for instance, the owner of a German cinema who had gone to Italy especially for the occasion was dumbfounded: "Fellini must be nuts! This is worse than *Marienbad*.[97] I couldn't follow it at all. And I'm supposed to show that to my audience?"[98]

The distributing company that handled *8 1/2* had been afraid from the beginning that it would meet with a lack of understanding. In order to reduce the audience's expected confusion, copies were circulated for a time in which the dream sequences were tinted to set them off, but the experiment was not well received[99] and it didn't change the opinions of some critics who had been confused by the film during the première. Dino Buzzati, for instance, admitted that he hadn't understood a lot of things and ended his review with the remark that it was "La masturbation d'un genie."[100] He was not so very far off the mark with this comment, for Fellini himself said in an interview, albeit many years later, that making films is a form of "intellectual masturbation"[101]. It's a form of intellectual pleasure many people must share with him, for there is no other way to explain the popularity of his films and the flood of awards they have received – in this case, an Oscar for Best Foreign Film, another for the best costumes in a black and white film, three Oscar nominations and first prize at the Moscow film festival, to name only the most important honours. One awards ceremony followed another and Fellini, who didn't much like such events anyway, decided not to show his films in competition in the future. But Fellini's stratagem didn't pay off, for his films were to continue to win prizes. Many years later, *8 1/2* won special recognition when the most important international film critics and historians voted it 5th on the list of the "World's Best Films" in 1982.[102]

If you ask Fellini what his favourite films are, he at first hesitates to answer, then tries to evade the question by saying he never goes to the cinema and doesn't know the standard film classics. But if you gently insist on an answer, he will mention a few directors whose work has impressed him: Ingmar Bergman, for example, with whom he feels a certain kinship, Akira Kurosawa, the Marx Brothers, Roberto Rossellini, John Ford, Orson Welles, Stanley Kubrick – a list of names that would be found in almost any film

Marcello Mastroianni as Guido Anselmi in *8½*, 1963

lexicon. If you ask Fellini which of his own films he likes the best, he mentions, naturally after some hesitation, *La Strada*, *La Dolce Vita*, and *8 1/2*.[103] *Juliet of the Spirits*, his first full-length colour film, is not among those mentioned, which is surprising since it is permeated by an atmosphere of the fantastic, which has always fascinated Fellini for its visionary power.

"I experimented with LSD."

Juliet of the Spirits is the feminine counterpart to *8 1/2*. Made after the latter, Fellini here portrays a woman's inner life. The fact that the role was played by Giulietta Masina was not a matter of chance, for if Fellini was intimately familiar with the inner life of any woman then it was with that of his wife. In 1957 he had already written a similar story for her: it was filmed by Eduardo de Filippo as *Fortunella*. If we consider the fact that Giulietta Masina portrayed women with whom she had very little in common in *La Strada* and *The Nights of Cabiria*, then *Juliet of the Spirits* could be considered a kind of recompense for those roles. And it is a remarkable kind of recompense, for *Juliet of the Spirits*, a film about the liberation of the self, went much further than *8 1/2*.

While a psychoanalytical interpretation is enough in the case of the last-named film, there are three more interpretive levels in *Juliet of the Spirits*: those of parapsychology, magic and drugs. Fellini had devoted his attention to the first two for some time, but the degree of cinematic realization in this film goes far beyond anything he had done up to that time. The experience with drugs, on the other hand, was new: "I took mescaline. I even ex-

perimented with LSD – in the presence of three doctors, a psychologist and a tape recorder. There was nothing unusual about the experience."[104] And it may really have seemed like that to someone who is used to living in a world of visions. In reply to a report in the French film magazine *Cahier du Cinéma*, in which it was said that *Juliet of the Spirits* could only be understood "by someone who was familiar with the effects of the hallucinogen LSD"[105], Fellini could only reply: "I don't need the stuff. I have visions like that without any help."[106]

With the completion of this film Fellini ended his collaboration with his friends, the writers Tullio Pinelli and Ennio Flaiano, and with Brunello Rondi, who had been at his side for years. Bernardino Zapponi and later Tonino Guerra were to take their places.

The reason why Fellini took leave, apparently without reason, from his long-time collaborators was explained several years later by an assistant to the director in an interview with *Newsweek*: "The problem is that Fellini, like all highly creative people, is egocentric. He unconsciously takes advantage of everyone who can help him in the creative process. He takes whatever he needs from a script writer and then goes on his way."[107]

"I thought this film was going to kill me."

Piero Gherardi, who was the set designer for many of Fellini's films, described his methods later in more drastic terms: "He latches on to every-one, drains them dry, and then throws them away."[108] Gherardi's harsh words were uttered at a time when Fellini was going through the greatest

Scene from *8½*, 1963

crisis of his life. It was a crisis that had already begun to shake him during work on *8 1/2* and now caused a physical and emotional blow-out. Federico Fellini, who otherwise seemed so self-assured, so vital and full of optimism, had been plagued by doubt since *8 1/2*. He began to question his professional competence all the more after the negative reactions to *Juliet of the Spirits*, which premièred on October 22, 1965. It soon became clear that this film would also be a financial failure, something Fellini had increasingly come to fear. Depression was the result and a kind of stubborn reaction that led him to invest all of his remaining energies in a new project, "Il viaggio di G. Mastorna" (The Journey of G. Mastorna). The film was never made, but the project came to be a test of Fellini as a professional and as an individual. With dogged determination he turned to work on the project, which was first financed by Rizzoli and later, after the initial contract had expired, by Dino de Laurentiis.

In spite of, or rather because of the doggedness with which he approached the project, he made very slow progress with his preparations. Though he wasn't able to see it, Fellini was constantly standing in his own way. While he was still working on the screenplay, sets and structures for exterior shots had been completed at a cost of over a quarter of a million pounds.[109] Months passed and Fellini didn't seem to be making any progress. Finally de Laurentiis began to get impatient. In the face of investments of this size he demanded concrete results – casting lists, for example, or shooting deadlines. But Fellini was still working on the screenplay. The situation grew ever more critical and began to have an effect on the film crew. Fellini's irritability led to a break with many people on the project who had been with him for years, and when de Laurentiis began to put pressure on him a quarrel broke out between them. The following letter from Fellini to de Laurentiis was written during this period:

Rome, September 4, 1966

Dear Dino,

I must tell you something that has been on my mind for a long time now and that has finally led to a decision. It's a question of a serious decision, one I don't want to overdramatize but one which is the only honest answer, to my mind, to the constant and unnecessary attempts to gloss over deeper and more authentic feelings for reasons that stem only from a feeling of friendship.

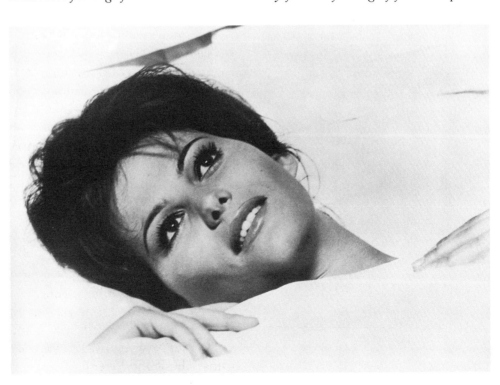

Claudia Cardinale in the role of Claudia in *8½*, 1963

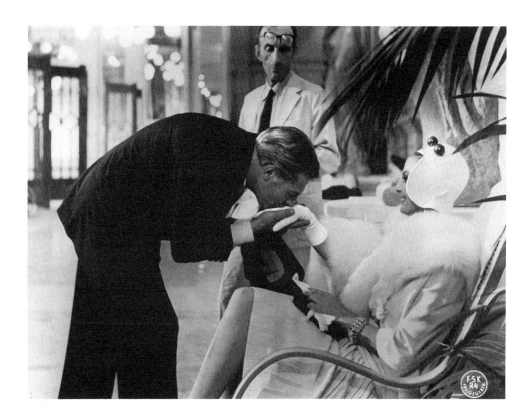

I can't start on the film – after everything that has happened, I wouldn't be able to finish it. Please don't misunderstand me: I have no doubts about the project, but a long series of contradictory and disruptive incidents which have nothing to do with the film itself created an atmosphere of resistance and hestitation from the beginning so that I have lost interest and no longer have the strength I need. Under these circumstances I can't make this film.

In order to spare you and myself embarrassing situations and unnecessary external consequences, and because I really need a little peace and quiet and time to be alone, I would like to ask you, in all friendliness, to contact Giorgio de Michele, to whom I have entrusted everything.

Given the friendship and respect that the long years of our relationship have brought with them, I hope that a way can be found to solve this problem.

I am sorry, dear Dino, that things have gone this far, but I can't change it. I embrace you and wish you well.[110]

At first the separation was not a friendly one, as Fellini had hoped it would be. De Laurentiis went to court and demanded 1.1 billion lire in damages, but the judge awarded him a total of only 350 million lire.[111] The money was supposed to be collected by a bailiff but there was hardly anything that could be seized at the Fellinis. The dispute continued until one day in February 1967, when Fellini and de Laurentiis decided to give it another try. The reconciliation comes as no surprise when we consider how much money de Laurentiis had already invested and the fact that Fellini had not found another backer after his decision not to cast Marcello Mastroianni in the lead. The role was to be taken over by the comedian Ugo Tognazzi. Even Fellini didn't seem to be completely convinced by his new choice: "One time", Tognazzi says, "Fellini even sent me to magicians to get their opinions about me. It was a kind of trial."[112]

Fellini was undecided about more than just the leading actor, though this demonstrates his confusion during the preparations for the film most vividly. At first Laurence Olivier was supposed to play Mastorna, then Mastroianni. Later on Fellini seriously considered Gregory Peck and Eli Wallach. At other times Paul Newman was just as much under discussion as were Danny Kaye, Omar Sharif and Peter O'Toole.

Federico Fellini, undated

Federico Fellini couldn't seem to go on – "Il viaggio di G. Mastorna" had driven him to despair and he had to admit that the film would never, could never be made: "Everything is blocked", he wrote in his notebook for "Mastorna", "everyone, even the audience, is affected by this paralysis."[113] Fellini's condition deteriorated visibly and depression finally led to a physical breakdown. On April 10, 1967, he was taken to the hospital with a case of pleurisy caused by an allergy. His condition was critical. "I thought", Fellini said later of "Il viaggio di G. Mastorna", "this film was going to kill me."[114] This should not be seen as merely macabre, given the fact that Fellini had planned to deal with the subject of death in the film. "Death", Fellini wrote in the screenplay for "Mastorna", "is so unfathomable that the mere thought of developing a theory is foolish and presumptuous."[115]

Once he got away from the studios and his office Fellini was soon on the road to recovery. He went to Manziana for a health cure and used the time there to write *La mia Rimini*. The book was not so much an effort to come to terms with the negative experiences of the "Mastorna" project as a reawakening of the memories of his home-town.

Though it was already clear to Fellini that he would not film "Il viaggio di G. Mastorna", he was still bound to de Laurentiis by contract. Only after a long dispute could Fellini convince his producer that it would be harmful to both of them to continue with the project. The contract was voided, but the only reason this took place as rapidly and as unproblematically as it did was that Fellini had found another producer who was willing to take over his debt. Alberto Grimaldi bailed Fellini out.[116]

"I can't stand myself anymore."

Fellini's rescue wasn't a matter of pure generosity, of course – his next film was to be made for Grimaldi's production company, which had agreements for co-operation with French producers. And there were already concrete ideas for the next project – a three-part episodic film called *Histoires extraordinaires* based on stories by Edgar Allan Poe. In addition to Fellini, the project was to include the French directors Louis Malle and Roger Vadim. They were, in effect, "left over" from a list of famous film-makers including Joseph Losey, Luchino Visconti and Orson Welles who were originally also supposed to take part.

Fellini wanted to use the new project to free himself completely from "Mastorna". But there were also other reasons for his agreement to work on the film: "I took on this project", he said in an interview, "because I thought – and that's the way it turned out – that contact with French directors would free me to find my own natural working rhythm once again."[117] It was a new beginning in many ways, with Fellini setting off in search of new ideas once again after a forced break of nearly three years. He had been given another opportunity to exercise his willfulness.[118]

The producers suggested that Fellini film the Poe story "The Tell-Tale Heart", but Fellini said he would rather film a novella by Bernardino Zapponi. The production companies rejected this suggestion since the film as a whole was to be based on works by Poe. Finally they agreed on Poe's tale of horror, "Never Bet the Devil Your Head – a Tale with a Moral" – which didn't mean that Fellini had given up the idea of Zapponi entirely. In co-operation with Zapponi, whom he had met and soon become friends with, he wrote the screenplay for his contribution to the *Histoires*, "a free, a very free rendition" of the original story by Poe.[119]

The script was ready in September 1967, and the only thing they needed in order to start shooting was an actor to play the lead. Peter O'Toole was

Fellini Satyricon
1969

Orchestra Rehearsal
1979

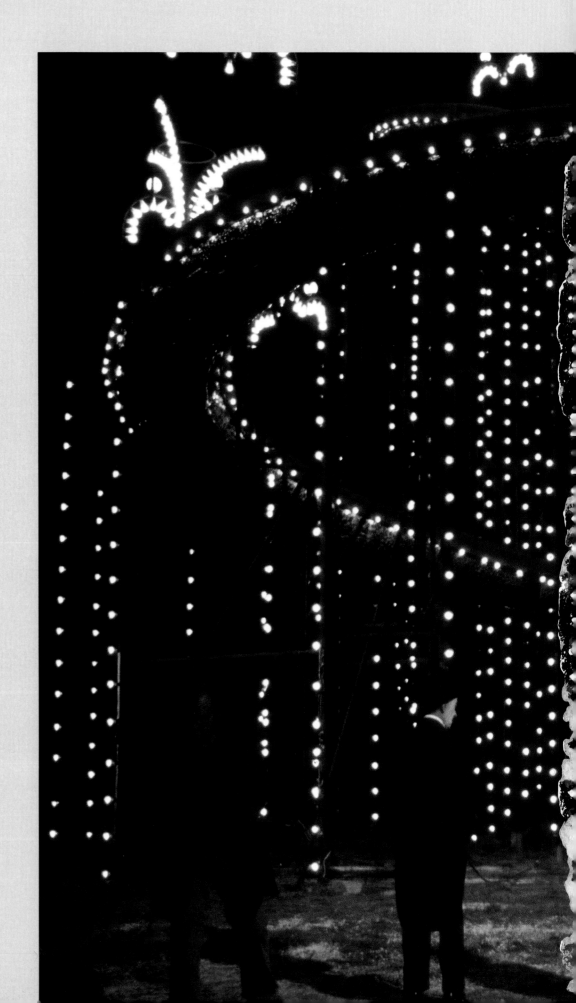

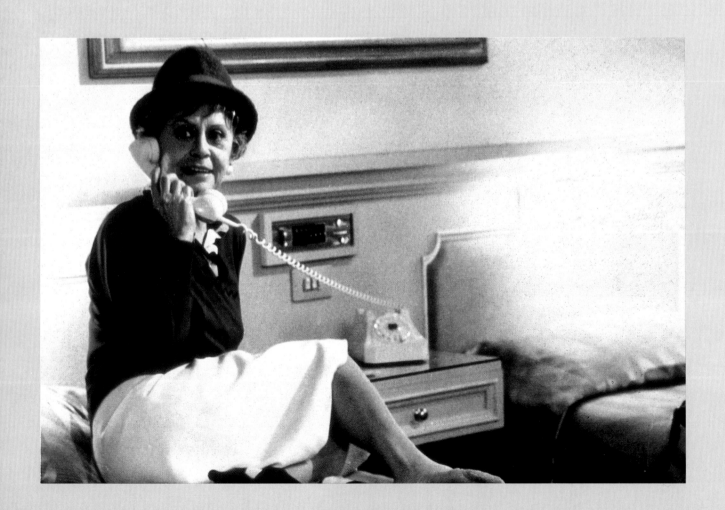

among those seriously considered, but negotiations with him ended in a quarrel.[120] Fellini kept looking and finally he decided on Terence Stamp as his Toby Dammit – the main character in Fellini's episode. Shooting began in December and took 26 days, an unusually short time for Fellini. But *Never Bet the Devil Your Head* was unlike Fellini's previous film efforts in other ways as well. He himself said of the film: "I wanted to exaggerate the Fellini style to the point of parody, until it was impossible ever to go back to it. I've had enough of my way of making films, with all of my banalities. I can't stand myself anymore."[121]

There can be no doubt that this statement reflects the after-effects of his breakdown. The dissatisfaction he expresses here was undoubtedly one of his main reasons for trying to get away from his old style in the works that followed. But while he wanted to create something entirely new, he remained true to himself in the end; more than that, he went on to perfect his style.

A Director's Notebook (Block-notes di un registra) was commissioned and financed by the National Broadcasting Company. What Fellini had hoped for in his work on *Never Bet the Devil Your Head* was realized during the work on the documentary film, *A Director's Notebook*: In the autumn of 1968 Fellini finally succeeded in freeing himself of "Il viaggio di G. Mastorna". By shooting the documentary in the ruins of the Mastorna sets and scenery Fellini was finally able to dispel the ghosts of his crisis and gather strength for his next feature-length film. Preparations for it began even as Fellini was working on the documentary.

Fellini was in his element. After the last take for *A Director's Notebook* in October, shooting began November 9th on *Satyricon*, a film based on the satire of the same name by Petronius Arbiter.

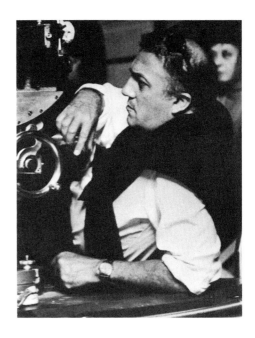

Federico Fellini, 1965

"Something completely unknown, deep within us."

"Why *Satyricon*? Why Petronius? In order to get started you need a good excuse. And for some reason, I don't know why, I used *Satyricon* this time.

I had read the book by Petronius many years before, at grammar school... The memory of reading the book had always remained very much alive, and it aroused an interest that gradually became a constant and mysterious temptation.

After a long time I read *Satyricon* again, maybe with less lustful curiosity than I did the first time, but with the same pleasure. The temptation to make a film based on the novel turned into a passion. *Satyricon* is a mysterious text, mostly because it is only preserved in fragments. But there is something symbolic about this fragmentariness. It is a metaphor for the incomplete knowledge we have today of the ancient world. This is the magic of this work and the world it portrays."[122]

For Fellini, the attraction of filming a fragmentarily preserved work from antiquity must have been that he could fill in the empty spaces. He had once again found something that stimulated his imagination. *Satyricon* is not a film about heathen Rome, although Fellini did research on the subject that went beyond Petronius' work, but a film about the way Fellini imagined heathen Rome. And *Satyricon* can also be seen as an attempt to approach a certain aspect of the theory of personality contained in the work of Carl Gustav Jung.

Fellini once said about his *Satyricon*: "It is ... not a film about the Roman world but about antiquity, and by antiquity I mean something completely unknown, deep within us."[123] A year earlier he had already been searching for this unknown something contained inside, but he hadn't been able to find it at the time: "Nothing occurred to me. Nothing at all... The frescoes of Pompeii? Herculaneum? – It could be that they say something, reveal something, communicate. I had only seen them once and I never knew exactly how much my fascination and enthusiasm were owing to the frescoes and how much to a magnificent Swedish woman who was walking in front of me. The emotional layer contained in these memories was buried so far down, covered by thousands of years of other myths and other ideologies, other fables and voices, that I never succeeded in making them vibrate."[124]

What does Fellini mean? He says his film is about an antiquity that everyone carries around with him, and he talks about an emotional layer full of memories that he wants to set vibrating, as if the same experiences and memories are present in the subconscious of every individual, experiences and memories he only needs to tap for his film. Fellini actually did work on this premise and he was undoubtedly drawing on the "collective subconscious" as Jung defined it in his theory of personality. Jung thought that during the history of man's development a memory of a special kind has developed. It embodies the experiences (archetypes) of all our forebears. On the basis of these special memories, of which man is unaware, there are more or less "innate" patterns of behaviour, for instance in the face of danger. Archetypes are often revealed in certain symbols, which then find their way into fairy tales, myths and religions.

In *Satyricon* Fellini was searching for such archetypes. He even looked for them at a kind of seance where he tried, with the help of a magician, a Fortune teller and a medium, to call up ancient Rome.[125] But since he didn't find them, he turned to a language of symbols that he felt corresponded most closely to the archetypes: "I used an iconography of allusion and non-reality of the kind you find in dreams."[126] It was clear to him from the beginning, however, that he didn't want to make a grand historical film.

As he has repeatedly said in interviews, what he had in mind was something like a science fiction film, one based on comic books like *Flash Gordon* but even more fantastic in nature. Basically, he wanted to do something that had never been done on the screen before, not in order to revolutionize the cinema but because this was the only way he saw himself in a position to realize his fantasies about *Satyricon*. Fellini had an idea for a long time of how his *Satyricon* should look, having already toyed with the idea of filming Petronius' work while he was shooting *The Young and the Passionate*. While he was working for *Marc'Aurelio* he was even supposed to have had plans to make a musical version of *Satyricon* with friends.[127] But this kind of treatment must have seemed too conventional to him in the long run and he dropped the idea. Established narrative structures were never to his liking, and during the preparations for *Satyricon* he even said that the use of such structures would be catastrophic.[128]

The biggest problem involved in making *Satyricon* was the question of the leading actors. Fellini remembers: "If I say, for example, 'Look! He has a face like a Roman!', then the person in question is likely to have the charisma of a bookkeeper or a tram conductor once he has been costumed and made up like a Roman. The head of Messalina as I know it from the Capitoline Olympus takes on the serene and benevolent features of a woman selling eggs at the market."[129]

Nevertheless he succeeded in finding the right faces, not least because of his unconventional approach to casting. For the leading roles, which were initially supposed to go to Terence Stamp and Pierre Clementi, he chose two completely unknown young actors, and the part of Trimalchione went to a well-known Roman barkeeper whose nickname was "Il Moro".

Shooting lasted more than six months, and the première took place at the Biennale on September 4, 1969. Once again a Fellini film left its audience in a state of confusion. Although there were those who praised *Satyricon* as

Fellini's best film to date, others were just as open in expressing their doubts about the work.

Fellini was repeatedly asked what he wanted to say in *Satyricon*, but as so often when asked about his work, he answered evasively: "I showed ancient Rome", he told the interviewer from a newspaper in Stuttgart, "but if you were to see a mirror of our own times in *Satyricon*, I wouldn't contradict you."[130]

Fellini has often said that *Satyricon* is basically a simple film even more than that, it is "very, very, very honest"[131]. But this is a characteristic that Fellini attributes to all his films.

Of all the countries in which *Satyricon* was shown and won recognition, its success in Japan was the greatest – it ran in one Japanese cinema for four years. Fellini also received enthusiastic confirmation of his work in a letter from Japan. The sender was none other than the master director, Akira Kurosawa. Kurosawa had already corresponded with Fellini during the filming of *Satyricon* concerning an episodic film that he was to make with Fellini and Ingmar Bergman. Nothing ever came of that project.

"The messengers of my calling."

Just as little came of Fellini's plans to make other features for American television. *A Director's Notebook* was broadcast in April 1969 and was so

Federico Fellini before a background of photographed Roman statues which play a role in the film *Fellini's Satyricon*, undated

Federico Fellini with Martin Potter as Encolpius
during filming of *Fellini's Satyricon*, 1969

popular with the television audience that the broadcasting company made
Fellini an offer for further co-operation. Fellini, who had a positive opinion of
private television at the time, was not disinclined and began collecting ideas.
He wanted to film reports on Mao Tse-tung, on an American factory, a day at
Fiat, on the Pope. With great enthusiasm Fellini formulated the most daring
projects. Even a report about a monastery in Tibet didn't appear to him to be
too far-fetched, although it must have been clear from the beginning that this
was all wishful thinking. Fellini was searching for a new film and, as so often
during such a phase, he simply gave free rein to his fantasy. After all, he hadn't
promised anything; there were no contracts at this time – and there wouldn't
be any in the future. At least not with American television, for Fellini soon
turned his back on it to make an agreement with the state-owned television
company of his own country, RAI.

Fellini's extravagant ideas for television documentaries were soon thrown
overboard and one Sunday afternoon, more or less over coffee and cake,

Fellini and Zapponi came up with the idea for a realistic project: *The Clowns, Messengers of My Calling*. We went to Paris looking for I didn't know what, and when we returned a few days later the screenplay was ready. To make a long story short, we had started without giving the whole thing much thought. I caught myself saying 'The Clowns', and later I caught myself making the film."[132]

In the work Fellini had done up to that time there had been many allusions to the world he now portrayed in his semi-documentary television film. He had never made a secret of his love of jugglers, acrobats, variety shows, clowns and the circus and a film that took all these things as its subject was really long overdue. Drawing on his first childhood encounter with the circus, Fellini expressed in the film itself what it was that made him want to make it: "The clowns from the ring, the clowns of my childhood, where have they gone? Does this rough humour, this deafening slapstick I once found so funny still exist? Can the things clowns did then still make people laugh? The world that brought them forth and of which they were an expression doesn't exist anymore. The circus of those days has given way to a racetrack. The naïve and colourful scenery, the childlike belief of the audience is gone. In today's circus you only find the last traces, and these traces are what we want to pursue."[133]

We can follow Fellini for a moment into the world of the circus to find out what magic it holds for him, a magic that goes far beyond what astonishes and makes you laugh. Like the Swedish director Ingmar Bergman in his film *Sawdust and Tinsel* (1953), Fellini feels that the circus artist has symbolic meaning. The clown in particular is, for Fellini, a metaphor for the artist in modern society.

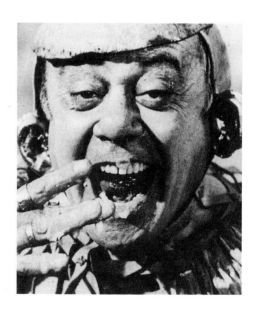

Fellini likes to compare film making with circus spectacle, and just as there are two kinds of clown – the White Clown and Dumb August – so he sees the whole world as divided into a clownish dualism: "The White Clown is something like an indisputable deity. He represents elegance, harmony, intelligence and clarity; in short, he embodies all of the qualities of a moral ideal... He is the papa, the mama, the master, the artist, the right thing to do... August, on the other hand, is like the tramp, the child, the vagabond, the drunk identified by his costume; that's why he can't wear anything else... The bourgeois family is an association of White Clowns in which the child has to play the role of Dumb August."[134]

Face from *Fellini's Satyricon*, 1969

Filming of *The Clowns,* 1970

If you ask Fellini which part he plays in the circus of life, he will first tell you Dumb August. But then he will say that he could just as well be the White Clown, "or even the circus director, the psychiatrist who has gone mad himself.

We can carry the game even further: Antonioni is an August, one of the melancholy, silent types . . .. Picasso is a triumphant, cheeky August who has no complexes, who can do anything. In the end he becomes master over the White Clown. Einstein is a dreamer, a fairy tale August who never talks but who at the last moment innocently pulls out of his sleeve the solution to a riddle the White Clown has given him out of sheer malice. Visconti is a White Clown of great authority. His magnificent costume alone is enough to intimidate others. Hitler is a White Clown, Mussolini an August. Pius XII is a White Clown, John XXIII an August, Freud a White Clown, Jung an August."[135]

This kind of thinking has constantly provided Fellini with inspiration for his films, and when, at the end of *The Clowns,* there is an extravagant funeral for Dumb August – representing the death of the traditional circus –, the images convey no real sense of sadness, for to Fellini the circus of life goes on, driven forward by the "clownishness of reality". The circus tent has been taken down to make way for the centre ring of everyday life.

"I want to see all the faces on this planet."

And Fellini is a detective in this circus, not only where new ideas for his films are concerned but with regard to the search for players. As far as possible he wants new faces for each new film, not stars but glimpses of the streets. Fellini always casts roles by physiognomy and, rather than work with professionals, he prefers embodiments of his imagined figures. If a star has the right face, fine, he can be signed – but not because of his popularity at the box office.

For Fellini faces are the "human landscape" of any film he plans:[136] "Faces are more important than anything else to me, more important than sets and costumes, more important than the screenplay and even more important than acting ability. Faces tell me what my film will look like."[137] They inspire him with regard to the action and the personalities of his figures, and he will sometimes even change the script just to create an opening for a face that he absolutely has to show in the film.

Ute Diehl said very aptly in her essay on Fellini: "In Fellini's films, with their constant trend away from action and narrative, a single face has always had to express fate, has always had to be the figuration of an idea."[138] What Fellini would like to do most is swim in a sea of faces, like Uncle Scrooge in his money, an invigorating swim each morning in a reservoir of faces: "I want to see all the faces on this planet. I'm never satisfied, and if I am satisfied, I want to compare the face I'm satisfied with against all the others, all of the other possible faces. It's neurotic."[139]

And he plunges into the subject neurotically, has photographs of faces sent to him, sends photographers out to hunt for faces, and is himself untiringly hunting, sighting, collecting, cataloguing. All that's missing from our Sherlock Holmes of faces is a magnifying glass. And he's proud of his obsession: "I have more faces in my files than the FBI."[140]

Scene from *The Clowns*, 1970

"When the money runs out, the film will be ready."

The Clowns was made in the spring of 1968 and was broadcast on Italian television at Christmas that year. The ratings weren't very good and even in the cinemas, where the film was later shown, it didn't draw a very large audience.

In terms of both style and content *The Clowns* points the way to Fellini's next two films, *Roma* (1972) and *Amarcord* (1974), and even, to a certain extent, to *Intervista* (1987). Apart from the fact that the story is told in a similar, almost journalistic style, the common element in these films is the fact that Fellini makes extensive use of his own memories. His childhood and youth have now become an inexhaustible source of cinematographic inspiration. Fellini creates a monument for all of the scurrilous types he has encountered during his life. But Fellini himself was the subject of such an honour even before *Roma*. In *Alex in Wonderland* (1970), in which Fellini makes a short appearance playing himself, the American director Paul Mazursky paid homage to his Italian colleague. *Alex in Wonderland* tells the story of the young director Alex and the creative crisis he is going through. Alex is a great admirer of Fellini and *8 1/2* is one of his favourite films. Mazursky is not the only director who has been inspired to make a film about his own work in the medium by Fellini's masterpiece. The subject of the "film within the film" and the confrontation with the problems that arise in making films have been the theme of a variety of works since *8 1/2*. These self-portraits are frequently an attempt by the director to settle accounts with the dream factory and with the directors' own ideas of what it is like. We need only think of Rainer Werner

Fassbinder's *Warnung vor einer heiligen Nutte* (Beware of a Holy Whore) (1970), Woody Allen's *Stardust Memories* (1980) and Blake Edward's *S. O. B.* (1982).[141]

Following his short visit to the dream world of Mazursky's protagonist Alex, Fellini continued down the path of his own wonderland. His destination was, as in *La Dolce Vita* and *Roma*, Rome, but this time not centred on any particular person. There wasn't even supposed to be an episodic narrative framework for the new project as there had been in his previous films: "Each part is as self-contained as an independent short film."[142] Fellini concentrated all of his affectionate attention on the city. Nothing was to detract from it, everything was to point to it. He wanted to capture its atmosphere and show what it was about Rome that fascinates and fascinated him, for his memories of Rome are also worked into the film – his arrival, for instance, and his first apartment in the city.

Myth upon myth. During the filming of *Roma* he added another chapter to the legend that had been woven around Fellini the film-maker. He admitted in interviews that he had improvised more than ever before in making *Roma*. There were more or less no plans and there is no thread running through the film. Fellini said that he was filming haphazardly. He claimed that he was not working under any pressure and that the only limits were those set by his financing: "When the money runs out, the film will be ready."[143]

And then there actually was no more money – the producer's bank went broke (though not because of Fellini's film) and shooting came to a halt. It was resumed and the film completed only in February 1972 after new financing had been found. Fellini had to leave out several episodes, but that didn't keep him from recreating a five-hundred-metre-long stretch of the Roman freeway system at Cinecittà. What Fellini made of this freeway sequence in his film is indicative of his need to reconstruct reality. Existing reality is never good enough and the reconstructions are never merely copies of actually existing models. Instead they represent the quintessence of these models. What it is that represents the essence of a thing can only be decided by Fellini himself, for it is his perception of things that guides the hands of his craftsmen. In the case of *Roma*, this meant observing in isolation in the studio every aspect of the city he wanted to show on film. And there were more aspects than he could deal with: "I had the feeling when my earlier films were finished that the subject was exhausted, used up by my treatment, bled to death ... With this film, though, I had the strange feeling that I had barely touched the surface. The material was not only not exhausted, it had hardly been touched ..."[144] Which is, so to say, nothing more than a promise to make another film about Rome soon. He made a beginning with *Ginger and Fred* (1985) and with *Intervista* (1987), but more or less in passing since each of the two films is really about one aspect of the city, television in the case of *Ginger and Fred* and Cinecittà, a city within a city, in *Intervista*. It was clear that Fellini would soon deliver another proof of his love for the city which he calls his "private flat".

But let's go back to *Roma* and the year 1972: "I often ask myself why I made a movie about Rome, what it was that inspired me to do it ... You have to know that I hate to travel. From time to time someone will suggest film projects that could only be realized by travelling. American television wanted to send me to Tibet, for instance, to India and Brazil, in order to make a kind of fantastic report about religion and magic ... It was, admittedly, a fascinating suggestion and I immediately said yes – knowing full well that I wouldn't move from the spot. My favourite stretch of country is the triangle between Rome, Ostia, and Viterbo. This is where I feel comfortable, so I could say I made a movie about Rome because I live in Rome and I like the city. But

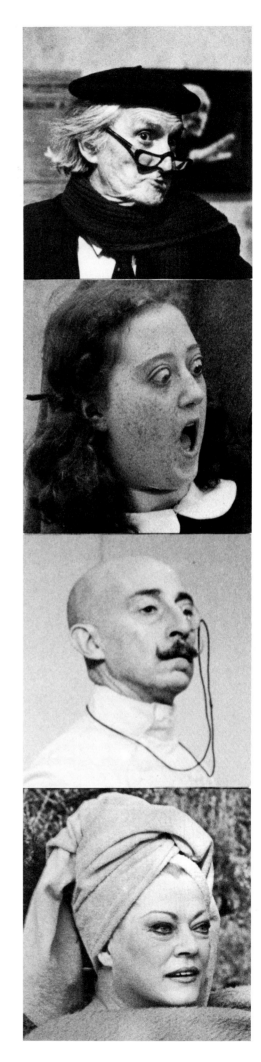

behind this obvious reason there is another one that goes back a long way. Right after *La Dolce Vita* Italian films about exotic trips were in fashion; *Green Magic* was just one of the titles. I said then, partly for the sake of argument and partly because I really thought that way, that you don't have to travel in order to experience the unusual, the foreign, the unexpected. Unknown aspects of life can also be found, or rather are particularly to be found in the things around us. An unexpected precipice, mysterious depths are more often revealed and felt with dismay within our own four walls and among friends. That's why I've been thinking since that time about Rome as seen by an outsider, a city that is close and yet as far away as if it were another planet. Beginning with this first idea, the project for the film developed in the course of time, almost without my noticing it."[145]

There actually is something alien, something strange about Fellini's Rome, although the images are pleasantly familiar at the same time, recognizable, obviously the products of a world Fellini had already created in his previous films and which forms the setting for his next work, *Amarcord*, more or less as the essence of the universe of his memory. There are certain clichés that clearly bear Fellini's signature: A woman, if she is a real woman – that is, if she is desirable-can only have large breasts and broad hips. The trademark of a man is his lustfulness, which he is constantly trying to satisfy for lack of any other activity.

To be a child in his films means growing up under the banner of Mussolini's Fascism. Eating, not only in the family, is a loud and chaotic rite of communication that sometimes ends in quarrels that look more serious than they really are. The bells of a church tower always hang threateningly over a visit to a brothel. The performances at a variety theatre are always embarrassingly amateurish acts performed for an audience that is rarely satisfied. The Church is the target of bitter sarcasm. Nature often seems like an emotional landscape ruffled by the winds of the search for knowledge; since night is an archetypal image of the origins of man, important scenes in Fellini's films often take place in the dark.

The world of Fellini's films is clearly structured. In previous films he showed us the kinds of lives his protagonists lead, and nothing is likely to change in this regard in the future. Life takes an orderly chaotic course in Fellini's work and, even if he is always telling us the same story, i.e. his own, more than almost any other director he always finds a way to surprise and amuse us – whether he finds a new detail among his memories that he just has to show us or because the physiognomy of a face he has not yet shown us comes to life again in his memory.

He sees Rome, too, as a face, as "big, reddish... that resembles Sordi, Fabrizzi, Magnani."[146] But this face doesn't bear their names. Fellini calls it "Mother": "Rome is... a mother, an ideal one at that, because she is indifferent. She is a mother who has too many children and, as a result, she can't look after you. She doesn't ask anything of you, expects nothing. She takes you in when you come and she lets you go when you want to leave, like the court in Kafka."[147]

Fellini's *Roma*, which wasn't very popular with the audience at first, can hardly be called Kafkaesque, even if it leaves the answers to many questions open, especially the one about the meaning of the ending. We won't get an answer from Fellini in any case, for he prefers to remain silent about the meaning of his films. Otherwise he is quite talkative in the numerous interviews he gives. Fellini loves to tell stories, a fact to which his films bear witness, and he has often called himself a "player in a puppet theater". The description is also apt in another way, for in every film project all of the strings are in his hands, and he moves his actors around like marionettes.

"I remember."

In his next film he had his marionettes dance to another tune. *Amarcord* is a seasonal ballet of memories in which Fellini tells us with almost shameless openness about his youth and, above all, about his home town of Rimini – though almost all the details are, of course, invented. Fellini had the idea for *Amarcord* in 1967 while he was on a health cure in Manziana, where he evoked the memory of his home town in the book *La mia Rimini*.

Fellini was able to win over Tonino Guerra as a collaborator on the screenplay, and he turned out to be a very positive addition to the project. Guerra, an unknown author and even less well-known scriptwriter, knew Rimini. He himself was from Sant'Arcangelo di Romagna, which is just a few kilometres from the coastal city.

The autobiographical aspects of Fellini's film are more than obvious and are even underscored by the title, which is drawn from the dialect of his own region and means "I remember". Fellini nevertheless stubbornly denied the presence of autobiographical connections for a time. To call *Amarcord* auto-biographical is "nonsense", he once said; "if I were supposed to make a film about the first things I can remember, then it would be a film about my beginnings at Cinecittà."[148] But Fellini's coyness about the autobiographical features of his films also works the other way: when you ask him about what he was like in school, he simply says "I have already told about my time at grammar school in *Amarcord*..."[149] And that's it. If you want to know something about this period, then you have to see his films, where he continued "his hunt for the making of a legend", as he put it, "without anger, without passing judgment and without bitterness."[150]

Like so many of Fellini's other films, *Amarcord* underwent a metamor-phosis during its making. Although it had been planned from the beginning to be a film about one man's memories, this look at the past was to be embedded in a kind of narrative frame set in the year 2000. The working title of the film was "The Violated Person". The plot was as follows: one day a man realizes that all of the people he lives with, who mean something to him, are basically strangers. "Strangers because they have lost a sense of their own origins, of the culture that has formed them, of their ancestors."[151] The man himself is going through a profound existential crisis, more or less as a representative of all mankind, as a result of the constant flood of stimuli to which he is subject in modern society. At the time Fellini said: "I can see how man is turning into a completely inauthentic figure, one who is in conflict with his own biology and physiology. Specialists have called our period the optic age. What is that supposed to mean? The image doesn't exist anymore, we no longer register it. We are bombarded by a constant and chaotic mass of distorted and false forms. We can no longer see, hear, feel, taste, or smell."[152]

The protagonist can only escape this loss, in the broadest sense, of his own identity through an awareness of his roots. And so he begins a journey into the past in the hope that he will able to make a new beginning there.

This narrative frame was not realized, supposedly for financial reasons. The money was needed for more important things: for instance, for recreating Rimini in the studios at Cinecittà, for a mock-up of an ocean liner, for a recreation of the ocean in the studios... "People always think I am very wasteful, doing all these things in the studios on a mere whim. Because it's expensive. People say that I work slowly. With busloads of people for walk-on appearances, and truckloads of film material. It's true that it took more than six months to shoot *Amarcord*, but what difference does it make? After

Scene from *Amarcord*, 1973

all, I'm not working in a Fiat factory."[153] And besides, he could have added that it was all worth it! Or was it? The effort was worth it in a number of ways. *Amarcord* got off to a successful artistic and financial start in Italy on December 18, 1973, and from there it continued its triumphal progress throughout the world, reaching its high point in 1974 with the Oscar for the Best Foreign Film.

Quickly forgotten was the fact that Fellini had gone way over his budget because of, among other things, strikes, illness and other incidents that had delayed shooting. And Fellini's portrayal of life in a small town under the dual influence of the Church and Fascism remains unforgettable. A banner that appears in the film more or less by chance gives trenchant expression to the social framework of the world portrayed in *Amarcord*: "Dio Patria Famiglia", it says – "God Country Family". The only thing that is missing is "Amore/Love", and the circle that forms the world of the provinces as Fellini sees it would be complete. Or should we say closed – Fellini often compared his film version of Rimini with a prison, with a place in which the ignorance of the inhabitants excludes the possibility of a critical confrontation with the Church and with Fascism. *Amarcord*, Fellini said, is a film that "confuses". It has a "direct relationship with the present day since it tries to call attention to the fact that the same social circumstances could recur, less naïvely and crudely but all the more dangerously. Fascism is like a threatening shadow that does not sit unmoving behind us but sometimes grows beyond us and

Maria Antonietta Beluzzi as tobacco vendor in *Amarcord*, 1973

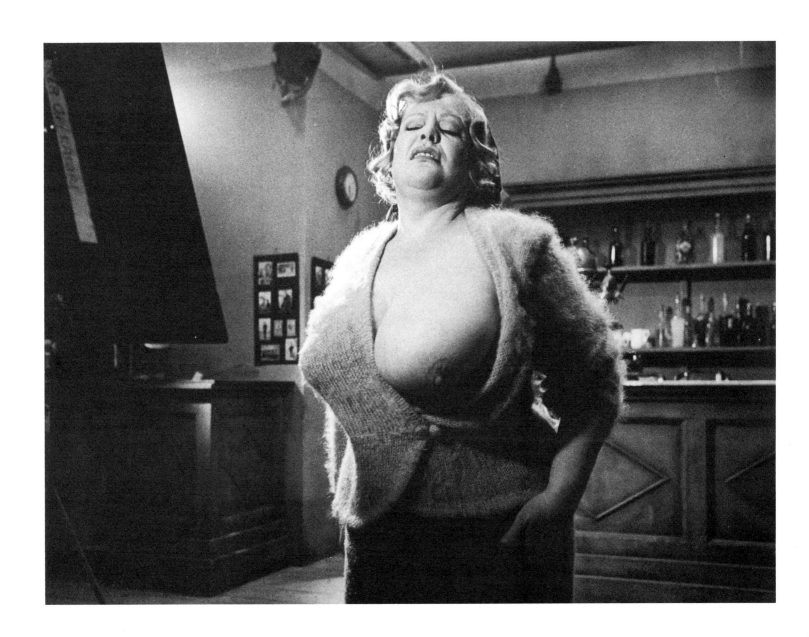

precedes us. Fascism is always waiting within us. There is always the danger of an upbringing, a Catholic upbringing, that knows only one goal: to place a person in a situation of intellectual dependence, to limit his integrity, to take from him any sense of responsibility in order to keep him in a never-ending state of immaturity. By showing life in a small town, I show life in a particular country and I show young people their own society. I show them how much fanaticism, provinciality, infantility, coarseness, how much disorder and humiliation there was under Fascism and in that society."[154]

The way in which Fellini ridicules the Fascists in his hometown in *Amarcord* reminds us of the sarcasm of his colleague Mel Brooks, who settled accounts with Fascism with an operetta-like treatment in *The Producers* (1967).

"This will be the worst film I have ever made."

Let's stick to "settling accounts", for it also points to what Fellini was up to in his next film, his own private settling of accounts with the myth of Casanova: "Casanova is a ridiculous, at most tragi-comic figure. I want to unmask him. He is the eternal boy who never grows up. To me Casanova is the typical immature Italian, the Papagallo, the heartbreaker, the women's idol, but in reality a mother's boy who rejects all responsibility and who lives in the pleasant illusion that everything comes from above; from Mama, from the King, from the *Duce*, from the Madonna. A man who is the prisoner of his own myths, including the one of being a heartbreaker."[155]
Fellini's revenge began with a tirade in many of the interviews he gave on the film. Giovanni Jacopo Casanova was for him a "dull writer, a trouble-maker, a braggart, an arsehole, a megalomaniac, a Fascist, a lover with ice-cold sperm, a human piston, a jumping jack, a provincial playboy, a blockhead." Fellini felt only disgust, aversion and hatred toward his 18th-century countryman. There were no points of contact, let alone of identification, with Casanova. He was the exact opposite of Fellini and there could therefore be no sense of kinship between the director-author and the main figure in this film as was usually the case with Fellini. The director's relationship with his hero was

Bruno Zanin as Titta in *Amarcord*, 1973

Carla Mora as a maid in *Amarcord*, 1973

disturbed from the beginning and this animosity was transferred to the work on the film.

Fellini was frequently heard to murmur during shooting: "I should never have made this film, I should have let it go. This will be the worst film I have ever made." And then he would give the following order to anyone who happened to be standing next to him: "I forbid you to go to see this film if it ever makes it to the screen."[156]

Why did he make the film at all? "The *Casanova* project is one of those things I have been cunningly selling to my producers for years, like *Il Decamerone* or *Satyricon*. With *Satyricon* it finally got me, after I had suggested it for so long, and I made the film and was glad I did. I wasn't able to make *Il Decamerone* because Pasolini got there first. *Casanova* was one of the three or four titles that I regularly used as bait when talking to producers: 'Let me make *The Young and the Passionate*' I said, 'and then I'll do *Il Decamerone*. Let me make *La Strada* and I promise you I'll do *L'Orlando Furioso*. Let me make *La Dolce Vita* and *8 1/2* and then I swear I'll make *Casanova*'."[157] It would appear that he also made such promises to the press. A newspaper in Cologne, for instance, carried the following note in November of 1957: "Federico Fellini, director of *La Strada*, *The Swindle* and *The Nights of Cabiria*, is preparing to make two new films – *The Spring of Love* and *The Memoirs of Casanova*."[158]

Another reason for filming *Casanova* was of course the fact that, after the completion of *Roma*, Fellini had signed contracts that bound him to the project. We can assume that this was the most telling reason for his perseverance. On the other hand, if we recall the commotion surrounding the aborted "Mastorna" project, then it becomes clear that no contract could or can prevent Fellini from not making a film if he doesn't want to.

Fellini has often said that he can't understand the admiration aroused by *Casanova*. But something about the Venetian playboy must have fascinated him, even if it was only the fact that he could hate someone so much. And then Fellini did take the edge off some of the aversion he had expressed at the

Scene from *Amarcord*, 1973

beginning in an interview he gave to Gian Luigi Rondi after he began work on *Casanova*: "The things I've said during the past two years have usually been foolish monologues. As long as a film is still floating in an undefinable atmosphere, wavering within the imagination, I have to charge myself up with aggression against it. My aggression is what brings it to life, routs it out into the open, insults it. It's a kind of ritual, a ceremony. Everyone has his own methods; that's what mine are like."[159]

When Rondi asked in return if everything he had said before about the film was untrue, Fellini answered: "I don't disavow the things I said. They gave expression to my original intentions and therefore had their reasons. But I wouldn't use them today in talking about a film that's already finished."[160] Not that he had changed his mind about Casanova – on the contrary, he finally realized what was behind his reservations about Casanova: his passionate rejection of the man was a last rebellion as he stood at a recognized turning-point, not necessarily in his career, but in his life. "After this film, the moody and unreliable part of me, the undecided part of me that was constantly seduced by compromise – the part of me that didn't want to grow up – had to die. For me the film meant crossing the line, gliding into the last part of my life."[161]

Federico Fellini was 57 years old when he said that, and he added: "...I'm almost in my sixties. Perhaps subconsciously I placed all my fears, the anxiety

I can't face, in this film. Perhaps the film was fed by my fears."[162] And this anxiety in turn created a sinister atmosphere that left no room for optimistic undertones.

Fellini's sudden recognition of his own mortality, suppressed for years by a creative joy in life, provided a fertile ground for sombre metaphors in which Casanova suddenly became a symbol for man struggling through life. His sexuality therefore had nothing to do with satisfaction but became a symbol for an all-consuming love of life.

At the end was a feeling of emptiness. Early on Fellini had spoken of the *Casanova* project as a "film about emptiness", a "film of death". And here is where we find the relationship with Fellini's biography, the point of contact with his new protagonist, a basis for identification. By making a film about a man who "constantly put himself on display and forgot to live in the process"[163], Fellini made a film about himself. It was an expensive one that used up three producers.

The first of these was Dino de Laurentiis. After the screenplay had been completed in the spring of 1974 and preparations for shooting had begun, the economic situation in Italy began to deteriorate.

De Laurentiis was afraid that the cost of making *Casanova* would explode and withdrew his money. The financing of the project was then taken over by Andrea Rizzoli, whose father, Angelo Rizzoli, had already produced *La Dolce Vita*, *8 1/2*, and *Juliet of the Spirits*. But the project also proved to be too much for the younger Rizzoli, and what de Laurentiis had feared now became reality. The actual costs of production went considerably beyond the estimates. Rizzoli got into financial difficulties, and this led once again to an interruption in production.

Only in January 1975, with Alberto Grimaldi, did Fellini find a producer who would remain with him to the end. But this didn't mean that all of the problems were solved.

At the end of August, for instance, a month after the beginning of shooting, several rolls of negative film done up to that point were stolen from a copying laboratory. That is, they were kidnapped, for there are supposed to have been demands for ransom money that were ignored. Fortunately the irreplaceable material was found a few months later, undamaged. But then came the next catastrophe. Fellini, who had reconstructed all of the settings for the film at Cinecittà "so that everything was more true than in nature but nothing was natural"[164], went far beyond his budget. He occupied almost all of Cinecittà for *Casanova*. Grimaldi charged Fellini with being a "wastrel" and called a halt to shooting on December 20. Only at the end of January, after a fierce dispute, could work be resumed. But the screenplay was cut and the camera crew was reduced in size.

The film was finally finished in mid-December 1976. *Casanova*, with production costs of over eight million dollars,[165] was the most expensive film Fellini had ever made. The film premièred in Italy but the opinion of the critics was largely negative and the audience seemed bored. Few people expressed approval publicly. One of them was Alberto Moravia, probably Italy's most famous living author, who was impressed by his friend's film. Moravia's French colleague, Georges Simenon, called *Casanova* a masterpiece and admitted that he had cried while watching it. Fellini himself must have felt like crying, though for different reasons. Even if his film was a great success in Japan, and even if the American film critic Pauline Kael wrote a devastating review but called Fellini an "Italian Orson Welles", *Casanova* soon turned out to be a failure internationally and the Oscar for the best costume designer which went to Danilo Donati could do nothing to change that.

"I don't have any answers."

Donald Sutherland as *Fellini's Casanova*, and Margaret Clementi as Casanova's sister Maddalena, 1973

Fellini's films have always provoked the most varied responses, and one of the things that makes him such an important director is that by breaking down taboos and addressing subjects polemically, he has led to their discussion, not only in Italian society. We need think only of *La Dolce Vita* or of his next film, *Orchestra Rehearsal* (1979), which led to a dispute even before it began its official run.

What was the cause of annoyance this time, one that surprised Fellini, catching him fully unawares, one which was amusing and at the same time alarming? The *Orchestra Rehearsal* had been commissioned for Italian television, a "little film", as Fellini often called it – probably because it had cost practically nothing in comparison with *Casanova* and because it was only 70 minutes long. This "little film" is, as the title says, about an orchestra rehearsal, at least on the surface.

Many people have seen in the chaos Fellini portrays a parable for the condition of Italian society, of the whole world. In view of the stubbornness with which this view was held Fellini, who at first rejected any attempt at interpretation, finally admitted that the film is a didactic comment about

living together: "The world today is in the throes of collective reaction, organized structures are breaking down and deep layers of the subconscious are being freed. My little film portrays a situation of collective confusion. The result is that everyone reacts to the confusion in his own way, giving expression to his fears and longings as he interprets what he thinks he sees on the screen. To call on the figure of a tyrant as a solution to the disorder, to accept in fatal resignation the incarnation of a new dictator, the archetype of the strong father who takes care of everything in his aggressive authority and who solves every problem, means to be afraid when confronted by the film. But it is also an expression of fear in language that is usually used for dealing with problems, i.e. the language of politics. The film portrays a state of madness; this madness causes anxiety, and there is therefore a call for the organized madness of a dictator."[167]

Fellini's view of the world, by nature rather that of the optimist, gradually began to grow more sombre. The personal insight he gained while making *Casanova* had left deep scars. The loafer Fellini, we might think, could no longer close his eyes to the social and political reality of his country. But in this we would be mistaken, for Fellini was always sensitive to what was going on outside the studios. We mustn't let ourselves be blinded by his frequently quoted remarks about being an uneducated man who just makes films, as someone who doesn't know anything and therefore has no answers. Such statements are mere protective measures to keep from being nailed down. For Fellini it is important to see things from all sides, without preconceived notions or ideas.

Scene from *Orchestra Rehearsal*, 1978

Fellini often said that his statements can only be thought of as approximations of what he means and feels: "I wish what I say didn't always come out sounding so didactic when it is repeated by other people. The danger of words is that they are always more final than the ideas that brought them forth – probably because we haven't found any words that are subtle enough to reflect a person's feelings in all their constantly changing uncertainty. Please don't try to find something absolute in what I say. I always try to express myself with certain reservations, but I can't always be sure that I say exactly what I feel or that I won't feel quite different after just a short time."[168]

To call Fellini an intellectual would be something of an insult in his eyes. He shouldn't really have anything against the word educated, though, for there can be no doubt that he is and that he reveals it in every interview. The question is only why he likes to play dumb. But he would probably just answer: "Don't ask me such clever stuff!"

Fellini has said as often as he could that he is not interested in politics. But to see his films as apolitical or as tales spun by a day-dreamer, by a narcissist in love with his own autobiography, means to have been blind and dumb while watching them. For even if Fellini has filmed primarily subjective or individualistic films, his works are always a reflection of Italian society and its development. Sometimes they are a distorted reflection, but they are always the artistic expression of reality, of a confrontation with the everyday world in all its forms.

Orchestra Rehearsal was filmed in the palace of the Italian president (a unique circumstance that caused a good deal of comment in society) and was

Scene from *Orchestra Rehearsal*, 1978

shown in a kind of pre-première to high-ranking government officials. This should lay to rest any remaining doubts, especially since the film is evidently a reaction to the assassination of the politician Aldo Moro in 1978. But if we look more closely at the rest of Fellini's films we will find in each of them a "political" reaction of this kind as well. In order to avoid being made use of for political purposes, however, Fellini avoids talking about his work in political terms. This isn't necessary in any case since his message is clear enough. Besides, Fellini is sceptical about the expressly "political film" and can't understand why film critics respond more positively, as he sees it, to these works than to others.

But what does he mean by "political film"? Fellini provided very important information for the evaluation of his own work in an interview with Martin Schlappner. His films, he said, "are not political in the way this term is usually understood, that is, as an immediately effective promise to change the bases of society by means of revolution. They are certainly not political in this sense. But if we understand "political" to mean an examination of the reasons for the fact that human unhappiness in its various manifestations has causes, if by political we mean injustice, if we understand it to mean that people are kept in ignorance through the abuse of power, if we understand political to mean that an attempt is made to give man back his inner dignity, to free him from ignorance and superstition, to give him the feeling that he has the right to develop and to know more about the world, if we understand all these things when we say political, then my films are political."[169]

Can we think of Fellini as just a silver screen dreamer? It wasn't just a figment of someone's imagination that he was among the directors who filmed the burial of Enrico Berlinguer, Chairman of the Italian Communist Party, in 1984. "Now listen", Fellini says, "I'm a citizen who lives in Cinecittà, so I can tell you something about this film city. I'm curious about what goes on outside the city, but everything outside is confused. I take what I need and carry it inside the walls of Cinecittà in order to turn it into a film. But I can't tell you anything at all about life outside the walls."[170] His films are all the more talkative for that, and it is irrelevant in the long run whether critics call them "political" or not. *Orchestra Rehearsal*, at any rate, is a political film.

Balduin Baas as director in *Orchestra Rehearsal*, 1978

The idea for the film had come to Fellini years before, and although he had always wanted to make it there had never really been a pressing reason to undertake the project at a particular time: "When they killed Moro I thought, now the time has come... It made a tremendous impression on me. Not so much the murder itself – I had expected that. But thinking about the deeper meaning and trying to understand why it had happened. What did the people who killed him really want? What had happened to all of us living in this country? Why had things gone so far here? There was no direct relationship between these questions and the film, at least I wasn't aware of one. Not during the planning stages but only much later did I become aware of the connection, after the film had been completed. Not that I didn't see the particular importance of the film from the beginning. It had just not become clear to me why it was important for me to make this film at this particular time. Later on I knew: it was the assassination of Moro."[171] Although the film was made for television, its première took place in a cinema at the end of February 1979; it was only shown on Italian television at Christmas later that year. The film was not seen by a large audience.

"A film about darkness, night, and water."

As *Orchestra Rehearsal* was being shown on television Fellini was in the middle of preparations for his next film, one that would cause as much commotion as his previous project, especially in feminist circles: *La Città delle Donne (The City of Women)*. The film had already existed as an idea for more than ten years; it was originally supposed to have been made as an episode in a work whose charm was to lie in the co-operation between Fellini and Ingmar Bergman. The episodic film was never made but Fellini didn't give up his idea, continuing to work on it with Zapponi until it appeared in the nightmare that cost nearly 5 million pounds.[172] Only a Fellini could have afforded to go to such expense in the middle of a crisis in the Italian film industry.

Anna Prucnal in *La Città delle Donne*, 1980

La Città delle Donne, which has frequently been criticized as "hostile to women", turned into a nightmare in more than one sense. On the one hand the confusing film spectacle has a depressing effect upon the viewer, and on the other, the making of the film was bound up with a number of catastrophes. The first of them was the death of Ettore Bevilacqua, who had been Fellini's personal masseur for a number of years and with whom Fellini had become friends. And on April 10, 1979, the composer Nino Rota died. With Rota Fellini lost not only a friend but the most congenial collaborator he ever had.

Nino Rota had composed almost all of the music for Fellini's films up to that time, and it had been more than just musical background for visual events. His music also went far beyond the usual measure of dramatic accentuation of a situation. Rota's scores were the musical expression of Fellini's inner world, of the nervous melancholy of the director that had to be released and at the same time kept under control in order to help breathe life into a film and give it Fellini's unmistakable rhythm. Rota's scores are the musical heartbeat of the director, composed always from the perspective of the knowing friend. The melodies are a combination of Fellini's wit and acceptance of life and Rota's dreamy reflections; they bring to life a mood and touch the most varied kinds of people, not only among the film audience but among Rota's colleagues in the music world. Rota's film scores have often been alluded to by others (for instance, by Snakefinger in his album *8 1/4*[173]), as well as played and arranged by various musicians (for example, Bo van de Graaf and Carla Bley[174]). Others have simply dedicated songs to him (for instance, some *chansons* by Katyna Ranieri[175]). But the greatest admirer of Rota's work is still Fellini, who says that he can't bear music outside the film studio but that he would listen to Rota's compositions for hours while creating a film.

Fellini's films without Rota's music are inconceivable and it is certainly no accident that Fellini continued to work with Rota's music even after the composer's death. Fellini seems to have established a working relationship with Nicola Piovani in the meantime, but the latter will never be able to replace Fellini's friend Rota.

In a kind of eulogy for Nino Rota, Fellini wrote: "Our understanding for one another was always full and complete. We didn't have to approach one another carefully, we always understood each other immediately. If I wanted to work as a director, Nino was already there. He was something like a condition for my further plans."[176]

But Rota's death during the work on *La Città delle Donne* was not the only one. Three months after the fantastic journey into the world of women began, Ettore Manni, who had a leading role alongside Marcello Mastroianni, committed suicide. His death forced the Gaumont production company to break off work on the film. Everyone who was working on the project was let go until further notice and plans for completion had to be changed, resulting in a delay of nearly two months. Only towards the end of September could shooting continue. But the signs for the film had not improved: in addition to a number of accidents on the set – Fellini himself was the victim of one of them and broke his right arm – there were two more deaths affecting people involved in the film; the mothers of both scriptwriter Brunello Rondi and Marcello Mastroianni died while they were working on *La Città delle Donne*.

"Some people are afraid of God; I fear women."

It is therefore not suprising that the film turned into a nightmare. But we shouldn't forget that the subject itself was reason enough for Fellini to turn to

Scene with Marcello Mastroianni as Snàporaz in
La Città delle Donne, 1980

sombre and chaotic visions: "Some people are afraid of God", he once said; "I
fear women."[177] The reason why the film turned out to be such a traumatic
experience can hardly be expressed more succinctly. Which brings us to one
of the key concepts in Fellini's world: the idea of woman.

"For me woman is the part I don't have. And since I don't know what I
don't have, I project onto her all my insecurity, all that is puzzling and
incomprehensible. The Swiss psychologist Carl Gustav Jung once said that
woman is to be found where darkness begins. Since the influence of the
Catholic Church keeps the Italian male from growing up, and since he is the
most incomprehensible of men on earth, he projects his great uncertainty
onto women."[178]

Fellini and women: a book could be written on that subject alone – Fellini's
fascination with women, his symbolic projections, the Madonna-and-whore
complex, his confusion, his anxiety, his obsession, his neuroses.

The only woman he says almost nothing about is his own wife, Giulietta
Masina: "The relationship between Giulietta and me is one foreseen by fate,
deep and unquestionable, one whose roots are hidden to me."[179] For more
than 47 years now, Giulietta Masina has been more than just a companion to
Fellini, she is undoubtedly his greatest support, "always a friend, a loving
creature who has always stood beside me in my work. We had a child, but it

Ettore Manni as Dr. Sante Katzone in *La Città delle Donne*, 1980

died at birth. I have never had any desire to get a divorce."[180] In 1974 the press carried quite different reports, and it was said that Fellini wanted to separate from his wife,[181] but their marriage has outlived crises of quite a different calibre. Fellini's affairs, for instance. Until 1980 there were only rumours, for Fellini was said to be quite discreet in matters of love. But in 1982 they were noted officially. Sandra Milo, who had worked on one of his films, wrote in her book *Caro Federico*[182] that she had been Fellini's mistress. Was she really? After all, she does call her confessions a "live fiction"[183].

Women. An inexhaustible subject, one that had attracted Fellini's attention for a long time, not only since his youth "but even before that. As a child I was surrounded by nurses, governesses, mothers, and women teachers. How else could Venus have been seen as the patroness of the arts? She embodies the goal, heaven, she helps one keep going. You have to admit that women fit in with the plans for this world very well. I couldn't have arranged things any better myself..."[184]

In interviews Fellini has often expressed his amazement that there is not a single woman, not even any talk of women, in many films made by other directors. This must really be surprising to him since he is convinced that all his films are basically about women: "I feel that I am entirely devoted to women and that I only get along well with them. They are myth, mystery, variety, charm, a stimulating encounter, a mirror in which to see yourself. Women unite all these things in one. I think even the cinema, the play of light and shadow, is a woman. You sit in the cinema like in the womb, still, introverted, safe in the darkness, waiting for life to appear on the screen. You should go to a cinema with the innocence of an embryo." And then we are cast into doubt about Fellini's view of women when he makes statements like the following: "The whore is the true mother of every Italian man. The figure of the mother is the basis of myth all over the Mediterranean. And we haven't been able to overcome this myth because it has never become reality. This is the reason why the whore, this sinister figure, has taken on such great importance. She is the one who allows us to come into actual contact with reality. For this, I want to express to the whore my honest and passionate

Scene from *La Città delle Donne*, 1980

114

recognition and gratitude. This creature of sin made it possible for me to experience life. She was the one who conveyed to me the deeper and more concrete meaning of life. Someone should set up a monument to the whore."[186] And that is exactly what Fellini has done! His work is filled with monuments that place women above men, with "some of the most popular figures of women in the modern cinema (Gelsomina, Cabiria)", as Tullio Kezich says.[187]

But whether they are whores or Madonnas, women don't have an easy time of it in Fellini's films. All of them must fight for the love of men, and it is a desperate struggle, full of longing and often meaningless. The women's liberation movement is probably not as upset at the representation of the vanity of these efforts as at Fellini's image of woman. She is either seductive and thus dangerous or she is what men consider the ideal wife, loving and caring and subordinate to her husband. More than thirty years ago Martin Schlappner found an affectionate description for Fellini's portrayal of this second type: Fellini would, he said, "drape these women in naïvity."[188]

For *La Città delle Donne* Fellini turned things around: this time it was the man who had to struggle, less for love than for survival as a man. While Fellini had exploded the myth of the male lover in *Casanova*, he totally destroyed the idea of male superiority in his *La Città delle Donne*.

Fellini wants to exhibit his solidarity with women and he does so by revealing to her all his anxieties. He visualizes his difficult relationship with women and in doing so reveals himself to be vulnerable.

Is *La Città delle Donne* Fellini's homage to his own fear of the opposite sex? It definitely is, but it is also something more: "The film is a man's journey through his own fantasy, the search for the self. It seems to me that an atmosphere of fear, restlessness, terror and sadness is quite appropriate."[189] Beginning with *8 1/2*, Fellini constantly returned to the same theme. But the apocalyptic note that crept in with *Casanova* reached its high point in Fellini's next work, *And the Ship Sails On* (1983).

"The absurd desire for a catastrophe."

Fellini had first outlined this film in 1981; now he set about work on it with Tonino Guerra, but "without much conviction"[190], as he later admitted. If

Renzo Rossellini, the producer, had not been so enthusiastic about the story from the beginning and if he hadn't urged Fellini to develop it, *And the Ship Sails On* would have disappeared into a drawer of Fellini's desk along with the other projects he never realized.

Encouraged by Rossellini, however, the team of authors set to work and completed the script within two weeks. The idea for the film was drawn from a short notice in a newspaper that Fellini had seen and cut out years before: "It said that after the death of an old Jesuit, an exchange of letters between the Jesuit and a retired Hungarian ambassador was found in the Jesuit's apartment. The correspondence had been initiated by the Jesuit, who wanted to satisfy his curiosity about the reasons for the First World War. And reasons came to light that quite clearly contradicted what was written in the school books. That was more or less what was written in the newspaper. Maybe I cut it out because I was moved by the realization that we have to reconsider what we first think of as historic fact and therefore pass on to the confusion of others."[191]

Fellini had a good deal of time in the months that followed for such reflections, for although the script found the approval of a colleague of Rossellini, the project lay dormant at first for lack of financing. This hardly disturbed Fellini since it gave him an opportunity to turn his attention to other projects he found more interesting, even if all of them were for television. Several series were under discussion simultaneously. There was the idea for a series of stories about Greek myths for an American broadcasting company, CBS, for instance, and for RAI in Italy there was an idea for a series of television films about a provincial lawyer and one for several detective stories with the title *Poliziotto (The Policeman):* "I want to hold up a mirror to our troubled times. I want to make palpable circumstances that seem like a labyrinth to most people ever more confusing, like terrorism. I think detective stories are a good way of portraying the labyrinth we find ourselves in."[192]

But he must have thought that a motion picture would be an even better vehicle for such an undertaking, for a labyrinth is much more threatening on the screen than it is on television. And so he returned to his idea of a ship of dreams. He spent the next few months looking for the right producer, an activity that had cost him a lot of time and energy for earlier projects but one that had always been successful. Shooting began in November 1982 with the backing of a consortium of supporters. Work was completed in 16 weeks at Cinecittà, which had been renamed "Fellinopolis" by the press in the meantime.[193]

In *And the Ship Sails on* (1983) Fellini set out on a jouney with a ship of the dead. The feverish expectation that filled the protagonists in *Amarcord* as they waited hopefully for the steamship "Rex" to appear is gone, as is the longing that came to life in the sea of lights from the portholes. The ship of dreams had long since set off on its voyage and with it went Fellini's optimism. In 1973 a ticket would have meant liberation. Ten years later, the nightmare ship "Gloria N." has only one destination – catastrophe: "We are filled with such a cold, rigid, soporific and impenetrable indifference that the absurd desire for a catastrophe secretly arises within us, for a catastrophe that could shake us out of our lethargy so that we can gain a new sense of reality and experience other possibilities. A misfortune that can make rebirth possible."[194]

Fellini may have grown more serious with age but he still can't deny his audience a ray of hope. In Fellini's fable our society is chugging along toward its ruin to the pompous strains of opera arias, but the "Gloria N." brings forth

Federico Fellini with his wife Giulietta Masina during filming of *Ginger and Fred,* 1985

Freddie Jones as Orlando in *And the Ship Sails On*, 1983

a Noah's ark on the plastic seas of Cinecittà that is radiant with the symbolic force of a last unicorn. As long as that exists man is not lost, even if the clock is about to strike midnight. As long as we can still dream, and the fabulous figure of the unicorn is a product of this imagination, the last hour will not have struck. *And the Ship Sails on* is therefore also a plea for the cinema, the now threatened (especially in Italy) scene of visualized dreams. Surprisingly enough it was Fellini himself who provided this interpretation of his work: "The film can also be read as a testimonial to the cinema itself. A film about the cinema, about what it once represented: a reality that was meant to bear testimony to another reality but that grew ever more distant from it until it disappeared."[195]

Fellini's open commitment to the old-fashioned cinema was warmly received by the audience and critics at the film festival in Venice, where *And the Ship Sails on* was shown for the first time on September 10, 1983. But the film enjoyed its greatest success in France, where it was considered a masterpiece. In spite of the positive reception of *And the Ship Sails on* by the critics, it didn't draw a large audience, a fate it shares, independent of the assessment by the mass media, with Fellini's last films. Tullio Kezich provides a convincing reason for this in his biography of Fellini: "Someone has advanced the hypothesis that the declining popularity of Fellini's last films is a result of the director's refusal to make his audience laugh."[196]

Fellini wasn't in a laughing mood, all the less so with the growing popularity of the private broadcasting company of the media mogul Silvio Berlusconi. It was not merely by chance that *And the Ship Sails on* was initially supposed to be about television with its flood of pseudo-information and its advertising mania. Fellini holds television responsible for the downfall of the cinema.

But Fellini had only postponed his day of reckoning with television. In *Ginger and Fred* (1985) he took up the subject once again, this time drawing on his own experience of the medium in the course of his career. And in his next film, *Intervista*, there was no lack of attacks on television.

"This kind of television doesn't deserve to survive."

The television adverts Fellini made for Campari and Barilla noodles after *And the Ship Sails on* were a kind of indirect preparation for *Ginger and Fred*.

Scene from *And the Ship Sails On*, 1983

Since he had spoken out vehemently against such work just a short time before it caused a certain amount of consternation, not only among his fans. Fellini is always good for surprises, but his turn to advertising is not one of them. Actually, this work was long since overdue, for where could he try out new forms of expression if not there? And the fact that he was always searching for such new forms is evident in all his work.

We can only speculate about the role played in this change of heart by money. The one thing that is certain is that the Italian film industry had been going through a period of crisis for years – it still is. And the periods between Fellini's films had grown ever longer. Although he had enjoyed international renown for years, his last films had not been box office hits and had been costly projects, with the exception of *Orchestra Rehearsal*. *Ginger and Fred*, originally planned as a 50-minute film for television, would finally run up costs of over 7 million pounds. Financing has to be found for such giant projects, and backers prefer a sure thing. But Fellini must have a credit-worthy guardian angel at his side for in the end financing was found for *Ginger and Fred*.

"*Ginger and Fred* is a film about our times, about my confusion and dismay at the fact that we live in a world in which we can recognize ourselves only with great effort. It seems to me that so many things have lost their value, have been destroyed... Everywhere you find uniformity, monotony and broad acceptance. Our lives are governed by stupid rituals whose content and rhythms are determined primarily by television and the media... The origins of the idea for *Ginger and Fred* are probably to be found in my irritation as I watched films on television. They are absolutely massacred by the constant interruption of adverts. No one respects the integrity of the work. As a viewer, I began to feel the desire for rebellion and revolution."[197]

Giulietta Masina and Marcello Mastroianni as
Ginger and Fred, 1985

First Fellini gave vent to his anger in written form. An article in which he gives rather drastic expression to his view of privately run Italian television appeared on December 7, 1985, in *Europeo* – its title: "This Kind of Television Doesn't Deserve to Survive":

"I don't have anything to do with television. It doesn't have any attraction for me, it doesn't arouse my curiosity. If I'm alone on a quiet Sunday afternoon, I change a burned-out light bulb or fix a lampshade, put my books in order or try to open a drawer that's stuck, stand at the window, talk to the cat next door – anything but turn on the television because that doesn't occur to me at all. Of course I've watched television at times and sometimes, if the television is on and someone at home is watching it, I watch it. But I don't remember anything afterwards, just like I don't remember the newspaper I read the day before yesterday or last year.

Some people might think this way of dissociating myself from television isn't very convincing since I've made films for television, even adverts. That's true – and I would even like to make more. But while I was working on the scripts and then shooting these films, while I was putting together the cast and the sets, while I was setting up shot after shot, I never for one moment thought that this was all for television and that everything I was doing was for this little, milky, blind screen. What I mean is that I don't think that television is a means of expression. At the most it's a means of distribution in which you can also show films, but only by limiting, humiliating, deforming them and reducing them to the format of a postcard. And all of that just to give the viewer at home the pleasant feeling that it's a little risqué because it's like a cheap form of voyeurism! It's like getting the first issue of a newspaper or magazine in the mail free of charge.

The constant interruptions of the films shown on privately run television are not only a form of despotism with regard to the author and his work but with regard to the viewer as well. You get used to the stuttering, gasping language, to interruptions of intellectual activity, and to all the little interruptions of concentration that finally turn the viewer into a patient idiot, unable to concentrate, to reflect, to make connections and to think ahead. And he grows dull to the feeling of musicality, harmony and eurhythmics that always accompanies something that is being told.

The viewer is a taster who always has his mouth full but can't taste anything anymore because he can't distinguish between one flavour and another. The only possible result of the distortion of every form of narrative logic is the creation of an endless audience of illiterates prepared to laugh at anything, to get excited, to applaud whatever repeats itself rapidly and meaninglessly.

Private broadcasting companies say that they need advertising in order to survive, but why should we worry about companies that flood Italian homes 24 hours a day with mad spectacles and pseudo-comedians who wouldn't have had a chance in variety theatre even at its low point in Cacini's times? Why should we be concerned about companies that constantly interrupt old films with crackling roasts, oceans of stew and armpits freshly sprayed with deodorant?

Burying the viewer under a mountain of advertising is a shameful violation, an act of aggression in a society that thinks people can live together on the basis of mutual consideration, that is, in accordance with the principle of self-restrained freedom: the refusal to intrude on the freedom of others or to harm, defile or injure them.

It doesn't seem to me that private television has any real arguments for disdaining or disfiguring works in which other people have invested so much time and thought. Criminals can also say that they commit their crimes in order to survive."[198]

In order to prevent such "crimes", at least against his own works, Fellini tried to get a court order barring private broadcasting companies from interrupting his films with adverts. His complaint was rejected by Italian judges.[199]

In 1989, after the death of the director Pietro Germi, his son was to fare better in such a case. After Germi's film *Serafino* (1968) had been shown by a private broadcaster with the usual interruptions for adverts, his indignant son filed a complaint that foresaw the prohibition of commercial interruptions of films shown on television. The first court ruling went against him but he won

Scene from *Ginger and Fred,* 1985

Scene from *Ginger and Fred*, 1985

on appeal in a Roman court: "Every interruption", the 30-page verdict said, "represents a change in the fundamental nature of the work."[200] This is in turn a violation of the rights of the author. Fellini said of the decision: "In the long run, the very long run, there is a little justice in this world after all."[201] Whether or not that is so in this case remains to be seen, for the company in question, which is part of Berlusconi's media empire, has appealed against the decision and the final judgment of the high court of appeals has not yet been handed down.

"It could be that everything that's been written about this film is wrong."

Ginger and Fred. Fellini's attack on television would one day be itself attacked. The American actress Ginger Rogers saw herself and her recently-deceased colleague Fred Astaire portrayed in a style and manner which demeaned their reputations.[202]

A strange reaction if we consider the fact that Fellini's figures have nothing in common with the Hollywood couple Rogers/Astaire except their names. The origins of the figure of Ginger are to be sought in *Variety Lights* or *La Strada*, and it is no accident that she was played by Giulietta Masina. And Fred is nothing other than Fellini's alter ego, played by Marcello Mastroianni, who has always played Fellini's most autobiographical figures.

While the black hat Mastroianni wore in *8 1/2* was enough of a hint at that time, since a black hat was more or less Fellini's trademark, identification is almost complete in *Ginger and Fred*. Mastroianni not only wears the same clothes his director wears, he is made up to look more like Fellini. The only thing that has been omitted is the flight to New York in June 1985 to participate in the awards ceremony arranged for the maestro by the Film Society of Lincoln Center (Fellini is the first non-Hollywood director to be so honoured).[203] Mastroianni could have worn the same make-up to the Biennale in Venice in September of that year, where Fellini was awarded the Golden Lion in recognition of his artistic work as director. But what does that mean? As if Fellini had already retired! At the time of the award ceremony he was busy synchronizing *Ginger and Fred* (which appeared in the cinemas in January 1986 to rave reviews, although the film was not to be a commercial success). Exactly one year later he began shooting *Intervista*, and in 1989 he

Scene from *Ginger and Fred*, 1985

was to begin work on his latest project, with the working title *La Voce della Luna (The Voice of the Moon)*.

In *Intervista*, which was at first planned only for television, Mastroianni once again has a part and once again, if only for a short time, turns himself into a surface onto which Fellini can project a very old longing.

Mastroianni embodies Mandrake, a figure from the comics that Fellini had loved since his childhood and that he had wanted to bring to film 20 years before: "Mandrake – what a wonderful subject, what riches! These picture stories have the kind of ironic distance that make it possible to treat the fantastic with just the right, healthy tone... There should be some kind of authority in Italy that forces me to make movies with Flash Gordon, Mandrake, and The Phantom. That would be ideal. Then I'd have a clear conscience. I would be forced to make these films and I'd be the happiest man alive!"[204] But Fellini can, after all, create his own pleasure, for although he is now 70 he is still full of energy and ideas, as *Intervista* and *La Voce della Luna* amusingly show.

"Directing without organization is nonsense."

Fellini has said that the film is no film but rather his life,[205] and there really is a good deal to be learned about him there. And since Fellini is mainly interested this time in showing how he makes a film, he doesn't have an actor substitute for him at all but plays, in all modesty, himself.

There is one point in his *Intervista* which Fellini will not go into: he does not reveal to the audience what film-making means to him. Luckily he has commented on that in other "intervistas".

Fellini, many of whose films contain journeys,[206] thinks of his work itself as a journey. Film-making is a trip with destinations that have been marked as if by magic on an inner map. Having reached one destination, he sets his sights on the next one not systematically but by chance. The script is like a suitcase "that you pack carefully to take on a trip and that contains everything you will need. But the suitcase is not the trip itself."[207] It is clear that Fellini does not follow a script closely and that his screenplays have literary rather than cinematic value. You can read them almost like a novel, independent of the

film story they tell. It's not surprising, therefore, that all of them have been
published.[208]

The script only serves to lay down in outline what the film will be about.
The figures are sketched in briefly, the scene of the action suggested, the
events themselves given in outline: "But at the beginning of a film I actually
don't want anything precise or well-defined. Work on a film wouldn't be any
fun then, it wouldn't be similar to life. If I knew what I was going to say, then I
wouldn't have to say it anymore, I'd be inwardly finished with it. That has
happened to me often: there are scripts I've written that I've never filmed
because the truth of the stories became clear to me and I didn't have to take the
journey through film in order to illuminate them."[209]

The actual film comes into existence during shooting and Fellini lets
himself be inspired by what is happening. Which brings us to the frequent
assertion in print that his work is pure improvisation. That is true only to a
point: "Anyone who knows a little bit about film-making, and especially
anyone who knows my films", says Fellini, "knows that there can be no talk
of improvisation."[210]

It would be closer to the truth to say that Fellini likes to incorporate chance
into his work. He remains open to the unforeseen and that's a large part of the
charm of his work, work that otherwise demands a considerable degree of
precision. Andrei Mikhalkov-Konchalovski laconically says in his interesting
essay on truth on the screen: "Directing without organization is nonsense."[211]

Fellini is aware of his destination before he sets out, but he is willing to take
into account unforeseen stopovers and detours. One built-in detour in every
film is the process of synchronization. Apart from the fact that the right voice
has to be found for the figures – the actors rarely synchronize their parts
themselves – the final definition of a character and of dialogue often takes
place during this part of the work on the film: "I add the dialogue only when
filming has been completed. The people in the film can do a better job of
acting if they don't have to remember their lines. This is all the more true since
I often use people who are not professional actors and have them speak the
way they would in everyday life so that they seem natural."[212] And if, in their
excitement, they can't even do that in front of the camera, Fellini simply has
them count. The process of synchronization then puts the right words into
their mouths.

"I don't think I could live without making films."

If you ask Fellini why he made this film and not that one, he regularly answers that he had, after all, signed a contract, that he had already received his advance and that since he didn't feel like paying back the money, he went ahead and made the film. Besides that, he makes films to "free" himself of them and especially because of his "shameful pleasure in telling tales."[213]

Like the author Franz Kafka (often an inspiration for Fellini – we need think only of *Intervista*, in which Kafka's *Amerika* was to be filmed), a man who could only experience his own life through writing, Fellini's work means everything to him: "I don't think I could live without making films."[214] He never thought of his profession as a burden but as the "most perfect and complete realization"[215] of himself: "My work is nothing but an admission of my longings and desires. It is the mirror image of my life."[216]

Fellini has spent almost his whole life tracking down life itself – not just his own – in films, at the beginning by analyzing its external conditions, later on with an interest in the inner truth of life. He has justly been called "a film-making psychoanalyst."[217] He is an analyst who thinks of his work as self-analysis and as therapy.

In their essay on Fellini, Wolfram Knorr and Marco Meier write: "In the triad of great film-making psychoanalysts of European culture – Bergman, Fellini and Buñuel –, all of whom (including his own modest self) Fellini admires, Fellini was always the most emotional, pursued and captured by the

Federico Fellini during filming of *Intervista*, 1987

devils of his own extravagantly powerful imagination, by dreams, demons, and loud and derisive laughter: hell's clown and hell's painter."[218]

"I'm a singer of street ballads in film."

To that we can only add that he is not only the most emotional, he is also the most subjective of the three. In the radicality of his subjectivity, he can only be compared with one other great film maker, the late Soviet director Andrei Tarkovski. In the works of both Tarkovski and Fellini we are witness to the almost incomprehensible visions of sensitive souls. Both directors make constant use of their own memories, which are heightened for cinematic purposes. Their messages are encoded images from the subconscious with strongly religious aspects, and both of them have an ethical interest in film. For Fellini as for Tarkovski, film as an art form penetrates to a deeper reality it is a microscope to be used in search of inner truth.

Tarkovski once called Fellini a poet, and indeed he is one. In 1983 Tarkovski wrote of his Italian colleague: "Fellini's being is realized through his own individual, subjectively defined and actively personalized world. The paradox of poetic creativity is that the more subjective the artist's view of the world, the deeper he is able to penetrate the objective facts of reality."[219] This way of formulating his ideas confirms that Tarkovski's understanding of his art as expressed in his book on film[220] was basically similar to that of Fellini.

The difference is in the mode of expression. While Tarkovski tends to formulate his ideas in philosophical and mystical terms, Fellini – in keeping with his nature – prefers to speak to us through caricature, avoiding all the while the pitfall of laughing at his characters. If we examine the concerns of these two great film artists, we see other parallels as well. Tarkovski was and Fellini is – to put it somewhat dramatically, interested in saving mankind, both in a physical and an intellectual-emotional sense.

This can be traced quite vividly in two figures that appear in their films and that bear a strong resemblance to one another. The two are philosophers who, in light of the alarming development of man, see an extreme form of action as the only way out. In Tarkovski's *Nostalgia* (1983) the figure is that of the mathematician Domenico, who has been declared mad and locked in for years by his family because of their fear of the madness of society. Following an extremely moving speech in Rome, he commits suicide by burning himself to death. Fellini's figure is named Steiner and he also lives in Rome, the decadent Rome of *La Dolce Vita* (1960). He also commits suicide, but only after killing his two children. This terrible act is, like Domenico's, a helpless and desperate outcry against the path man has taken.

In contrast to Tarkovski, for whom the salvation of man is possible if each individual brings his actions into harmony with his conscience, Fellini can recommend no solutions: "The only thing I can offer my figures, who are always filled with unhappiness, is solidarity – I can tell them: Listen, I can't explain what has gone wrong, but I'll stay here with you and sing you a song."[221]

Fellini wants to give those marked by fate a ray of hope, not by pretending that there's a happy end – there are none in real life – but by supplying, as it were, food for thought. The people in his audience are supposed to begin to think about themselves and their relations with others, for there is a great deal that is out of order there. But what is out of order is not innate, it is passing in nature. That is, passing if something is done to counter it. Fellini has shown repeatedly in his films where we have to start. Recognition of the loneliness of the individual runs like a thread throughout his work, not the meaninglessness of existence in and of itself but of the way we shape it. Many of Fellini's protagonists are profoundly melancholy. They are, and some of them suspect it – for instance Moraldo in *The Young and the Passionate* – the driftwood carried along by their own lack of a sense of meaning, victims of socially dictated isolation. In order to change anything, they must first break through their own resignation.

In his first films, Fellini allowed his figures to do just that. We need think only of Moraldo in *The Young and the Passionate* or Zampano in *La Strada*. Such an act of liberation is the exception in Fellini's later works, where sombre thoughts have shaken his optimism and his belief in the good in man. The hope and faith that emanate from *Intervista* didn't stay with him long. And so, with *La Voce della Luna*, Fellini returns to the dismal visions which belong to a doomed world. Although it seemed, at the end of the 80's, as if he had participated in a seminar on Positive Thinking.

After *Ginger and Fred*, which dealt in part with sorrow over the decline of the cinema, Fellini did not resign; rather, he filmed *Intervista*, the other side of the autobiographical aspects of a life-long homage to the cinema. This turned out to be a declaration of love to all the innumerable members of his staff, a declaration of love to all the bit players and extras and especially to Cinecittà, this primal nothingness from which Fellini created the "All" of his films.

Intervista, which was awarded a special prize at the Cannes Film Festival in 1987, as well as the Audience Award and Grand Prize at the Moscow Film Festival, is often described as one of Fellini's "later works". The problem is, it doesn't contain any of the qualities associated with an artist's later works. *Intervista* is colourful, loud, witty, quick, fresh, temperamental and, above all, optimistic – without lacking depth.

Federico Fellini with Anita Ekberg and Marcello Mastroianni during filming of *Intervista*, 1987

"I came along like Buster Keaton as a railroad engine driver."[222]

Fellini's most recent film, *La Voce della Luna*, looks much more like a "later work" and indeed like a later work which fulfils the maestro's often and gladly expressed opinion that he always just remakes the same film. *La Voce della Luna* unfortunately has nothing new to say to us. The icons of Fellini's melancholy cosmos have become too familiar, the wise sayings of his protagonists too trite. The film runs like a revue number that one loves because one knows it so well, but about which one eventually realizes that the dancers have all become old and the entertainers' jokes are no longer amusing. And then: why not go outside and catch the real-life clowning around? There one would without a doubt find all the Felliniesque faces that the maestro can no longer show us with his new film. The appearance of his sleepwalkers seems like transfer pictures of great Felliniesque stereotypes; the action is reduced to a reflection of episodic stories with which Fellini used to write film scripts.

It is astounding that, especialy with *La Voce della Luna*, he could come up with a money-maker in Italy where his last films have all been flops. The film, which cost nearly ten million pounds to make,[223] took in over one million pounds in its first four days of release in nearly 150 cinemas.[124] This financial success cannot be explained solely by the fact that Fellini once again succeeded in producing scenes of pure poetry, scenes which visualize the hovering stillness of madness and which, full of tender magic, give us a hint of what this film could have been.

If one disregards the endless tape-loop of Felliniesque ingredients which become fossilized clichés, then a view opens up of a visionary game – at the centre of which stands the delivery of the moon to a lunatic asylum. Delivery with a double meaning. First the moon creates all the voices that the protagonist (actually, Marcello Mastroianni should have played this part) hears and which drive him on to search for the indescribable. Then, however, the moon is personally lowered to earth and captured by three craftsmen so that it can give the answer to the Question of All Questions to mankind. But the moon, naturally a symbol for Woman, who for Fellini will always be an alien planet, makes a sad face, for in response to the question of the meaning of life she can only give one answer: And now for a word from our sponsor...

This wouldn't, however, represent advertising as in *Ginger and Fred* or *Intervista*. Even the production of Fellini's hatred of advertising itself doesn't really ignite. But perhaps this is all because, in order to make *La Voce della Luna*, he had to leave his beloved Cinecittà in order to work at Dinocittà, the film studios of his old friend Dino de Laurentiis. "...this time I had no choice but to come here", comments Fellini regarding his decision. "I needed wide open spaces. And everything around Cinecittà has long been built up."[225] One might almost have the impression that Fellini is disappointed that he, with his skyscrapers of vision and memory, had not built up the area around Cinecittà himself. But he has no reason to be sad. He will leave enough monuments to the world of night. His films tower above the low buildings of the present-day film industry, even though he may have botched things up with *La Voce della Luna* in giving us "typicalness" that is rather atypical Fellini.

Typical/atypical – one should not use this kind of classification regarding his works. Fellini himself rejects such considerations outright. There is, however, one category to which, in my opinion, his collected works belong: worth seeing.

Federico Fellini, 1984

Notes

1) Fellini, quoted from Teja Fiedler, Beatrice Schlag and Gerald Sturz, "Ohne Frauen gibt es keinen Zauber", *Stern*, November 5, 1987, p. 80

2) Federico Fellini, *Aufsätze und Notizen*, ed. Anna Keel and Christian Strich, Diogenes Verlag, Zürich, 1981, p. 65

3) Ibid., p. 146

4) Fellini, quoted from Sonja Schoonejans, *Fellinis Stadt der Frauen*, Wilhelm Heyne Verlag, Munich, 1980, p. 149

5) See Tullio Kezich, *Fellini – Eine Biographie*, Diogenes Verlag, Zürich, 1989, pp. 28 f.

6) See Giovanni Grazzini, *Warum machen Sie nicht mal eine schöne Liebesgeschichte?*, Diogenes Verlag, Zürich, 1984, pp. 15 f.

7) Fellini, quoted from *Amarcord*, Diogenes Verlag, Zürich, 1974, pp. 308 ff.

8) See Grazzini, *Warum . . .*, p. 13

9) Fellini, quoted from Gideon Bachmann, "Federico Fellini" in Ulrich Gregor, ed., *Wie sie filmen*, Sigbert Mohn Verlag, Gütersloh, 1966, p. 60

10) See Grazzini, *Warum . . .*, p. 74

11) Fellini, quoted from Martin Schlappner, *Von Rossellini zu Fellini*, Origo Verlag, Zürich, 1958, p. 245

12) Fellini, quoted from ibid., pp. 245 f.

13) Fellini, quoted from Grazzini, *Warum . . .*, p. 23

14) Fellini, quoted from Deena Boyer, *Die 200 Tage von 8 1/2*, Rowohlt Taschenbuch Verlag, Hamburg, 1963, pp. 129 ff.

15) Fellini, quoted from Armin Halstenberg, "Ich bin kein Messias," *Kölner Stadt Anzeiger*, March 7, 1970

16) Fellini, quoted from Grazzini, *Warum . . .*, p. 33

17) Fellini, quoted from ibid., p. 34

18) Fellini, *Aufsätze . . .*, p. 28

19) See Kezich, Fellini . . ., p. 48

20) Fellini, quoted from Michael Caen and Francis Lacassin, "Fellini und die Comics," *film*, no. 2, 1965, p. 26

21) Fellini, quoted from Costanzo Costantini in *Playboy*, no. 5, May 1981, p. 76

22) Fellini, quoted from Franco Pecori, *Federico Fellini*, 2nd ed., La Nuova Italia Editrice, Florence, 1978, p. 3

23) Fellini, *Aufsätze . . .*, p. 63

24) Ibid.

25) See Kezich, Fellini . . ., p. 143

26) Fellini, quoted from Grazzini, *Warum . . .*, p. 43

27) See Kezich, Fellini . . ., p. 135

28) See ibid., 159

29) See Grazzini, *Warum . . .*, p. 51

30) See Claudio G. Fava and Aldo Vigano, *i film di Federico Fellini*, Gremese Editore, Rome, 1987, p. 28

31) Fellini, quoted from Grazzini, *Warum . . .*, pp. 51f.

32) Kezich, *Fellini . . .*, p. 168

33) Fellini, quoted from Melton S. Davis, "Filmemacher Federico Fellini," *Das Beste*, No. 8, August 1972, p. 51. Kezich also reports a telephone conversation in his book, but the content is different. According to Kezich, Fellini asked Masina for a photograph that he could pass on to a film company for casting assignments (see Kezich, *Fellini . . .*, p. 115)

34) Fellini, quoted from Davis, *Filmemacher . . .*, p. 51

35) Fellini, *Aufsätze . . .*, p. 57

36) See Peter W. Jansen and Wolfram Schütte (eds.), "Roberto Rossellini", *Reihe Film* no. 36, Carl Hanser Verlag, Munich 1987, p. 270

37) Fellini, *Aufsätze . . .*, p. 61

38) Fellini, quoted from Pecori, *Federico Fellini*, p. 4

39) Zavattini, quoted from Oskar Kalbus, *Filme der Gegenwart*, Ewalt Skulima Verlag, Heidelberg, 1957, p. 364

40) Nini Ghelli, quoted from *Aspekte des italienischen Films*, vol. I, Verband der deutschen Filmclubs e.V., 1969, p. 62

41) See Kezich, *Fellini . . .*, p. 244

42) Fellini, quoted from Grazzini, *Warum . . .*, p. 56

43) Federico Fellini, *Lo sceicco bianco*, Garzanti Editori, 1980, p. 8

44) Fellini, quoted from Wolfram Knorr and Marco Meier, "Ich bin ein ungebildeter Mensch und mache Filme", *Die Weltwoche*, January 26, 1984, p. 37

45) Bogdanovich, quoted from Carter S. Wiseman and Edward Behr, "Magician of the Movies", *Newsweek*, August 18, 1975, p. 43

46) See Kezich, *Fellini . . .*, p. 296. Kezich refers to *Calle Mayor* (1956) by Juan Antonio Bardem, *I basilischi* (1963) by Lina Wertmüller, and, rightly enough, *Mean Streets* (1973) by Martin Scorsese and *American Graffiti* (1974) by George Lucas.

47) Luigi Marcorelli and Mario Verdone, "Neorealismus oder Hollywood am Tiber?", *Der Film in Europa*, Dokumenta Verlag Offenburg in Baden, 1955, p. 61

48) Fellini, quoted from Grazzini, *Warum . . .*, p. 88

49) Fellini, quoted from "Ein gewisses Lächeln", *Der Spiegel*, February 26, 1958, p. 50

50) Giulietta Masina, quoted from ibid.

51) See the report of a critic cited in Kezich, *Fellini . . .*, p. 325

52) Cayatte, quoted from Grazzini, *Warum . . .*, p. 90

53) See Fellini, "The Bitter Life – Of Money" in Harry M. Geduld, *Film Makers on Film Making*, Indiana University Press, Bloomington and London, 1967, p. 192

54) See Kezich, *Fellini . . .*, p. 333

55) The music is available through the import service of Emi Electrola

56) See Fava and Vigano, *i film . . .*, p. 32

57) Fellini, *Aufsätze . . .*, pp. 85 ff.

58) Fellini, quoted from Pecori, *Federico Fellini*, pp. 5 ff.

59) See Schlappner, *Von Rossellini . . .*, p. 269

60) See Wilfried Wiegand, "Federico Fellini", *Frankfurter Allgemeine Magazin*, June 15, 1984

61) Fellini, quoted from Michael Hanisch, "Erinnerung und Phantasie" in Horst Knietzsch (ed.), *Prisma, Kino- und Fernsehalmanach*, No. 16, Henschelverlag Kunst und Gesellschaft, Berlin, 1985, p. 203

62) See, e.g.:
– Waldemar Lilli, *Soziale Akzentuierung*, 1975;
– Sergei L. Rubinstein, *Sein und Bewußtsein*, 1983;
– Adam Schaff, *Stereotypen und das menschliche Handeln*, 1980

63) Fellini, quoted from Bert Reisfeld, "Ein meisterhafter Alptraum", *Stuttgarter Zeitung*, January 23, 1970

64) Liliana Betti, *Fellini*, Diogenes Verlag, Zürich, 1980, p. 57

65) Fellini, *Aufsätze . . .*, p. 69

66) See Pecori, *Federico Fellini*, pp. 57 ff.

67) Kezich, *Fellini . . .*, pp. 348 f.

68) See Fava and Vigano, *i film . . .*, p. 34

69) Federico Fellini, *Die Nächte der Cabiria*, Diogenes Verlag, Zürich, 1977, p. 155

70) See *Aspekte des italienischen Films*, pp. 2 ff.

71) Quoted from "Ein gewisses Lächeln", *Der Spiegel . . .*, p. 47

72) Fellini, *Aufsätze . . .*, p. 101

73) See "Das süße Leben", *Der Spiegel*, February 17, 1960, p. 73

74) Fellini, *Aufsätze . . .*, p. 102

75) Fava and Vigano, *i film . . .*, p. 36

76) Grazzini, *Warum . . .*, p. 113

77) Federico Fellini, *La dolce vita*, Diogenes Verlag, Zürich, 1974, p. 191

78) See Kezich, *Fellini . . .*, p. 426

79) See Hans Scheugl and Ernst Schmidt jr., *Lexikon des Avantgarde-, Experimental- und Undergroundfilms*, vol. I, Suhrkamp Verlag, 1974, pp. 381 f.

80) Fellini, *The Bitter Life . . .*, p. 193

81) Pasolini, quoted from Enzo Siciliano, *Pasolini – Leben und Werk*, Beltz & Gelberg, Weinheim, 1980, p. 290

82) Fellini, *Aufsätze . . .*, p. 68

83) See Samuel Fuller in the film *Der Stand der Dinge* (1982) by Wim Wenders

84) Fellini, quoted from Bachmann, "Federico Fellini" in Gregor (ed.), *Wie sie filmen*, p. 75

85) Fellini, quoted from Boyer, *Die 200 Tage . . .*, p. 14

86) Fellini, quoted from ibid.

87) Fellini, *Aufsätze . . .*, p. 188

88) See Ute Diehl, "Ich, Federico, Kaiser und Clown", *Westermanns Monatshefte*, March, 1973, p. 46

89) See Calvin S. Hall and Gardner Lindzey, *Theorien der Persönlichkeit*, vol. I, Verlag C.H. Beck, Munich, 1978, pp. 98–136

90) Fellini, *Achteinhalb*, Diogenes Verlag, Zürich, 1974, p. 149

91) Fellini, quoted from ibid., p. 168

92) *Handbuch VII der Katholischen Filmkritik*, Verlag Haus Altenberg, Düsseldorf, 1965, p. 10

93) Fellini, quoted from "Asa NIsi MAsa", *Der Spiegel*, November 28, 1962

94) See Boyer, *Die 200 Tage . . .*, pp. 144 ff.

95) Quoted from "Asa NIsi MAsa", *Der Spiegel . . .*

96) Eric Rhode, "Fellini's Double City", *Encounter*, June, 1964, p. 44

97) The allusion is to *L'année dernière à Marienbad* (Last Year at Marienbad), which was made in 1960 by Alain Resnais

98) Quoted from "Fellini 8 1/2 – Pressestimmen zur Uraufführung", *film*, 1/1963, p. 41

99) See Fava and Vigano, *i film . . .*, p. 38

100) Buzzati, quoted from "Fellini 8 1/2 – Pressestimmen . . .", p. 41

101) See Schoonejans, *Fellinis Stadt der Frauen*, p. 79

102) The best international films and their directors were:
1. Citizen Kane (1941), Orson Welles
2. La règle du jeu (The Rules of the Game) (1939), Jean Renoir
3. Shichinin no samurai (The Seven Samurai) (1954), Akira Kurosawa
4. Singin' in the Rain (1952), Stanley Donen and Gene Kelly
5. *8 1/2* (1963), Federico Fellini
6. Bronensets Potyomkin (Battleship Potemkin) (1925), Sergei Eisenstein
7. L'avventura (1960), Michelangelo Antonioni
8. The Magnificent Ambersons (1942), Orson Welles
9. Vertigo (1958), Alfred Hitchcock
10. The General (1926), Buster Keaton/Clyde Bruckman
11. The Searchers (1956), John Ford
Films that received the same number of votes were given the same position in the rating. Source: Warner-Columbia Distributors

103) See Richard Lacayo, "A World Going Down the Tube", *Time*, no. 4 (January 27, 1986), p. 31

104) Fellini, *Satyricon*, p. 233

105) Quoted from "Drang zur Droge", *Der Spiegel*, no. 37, September 5, 1966

106) Fellini, quoted from ibid.

107) Gerald Morin, quoted from Wiseman and Behr, *The Magician . . .*, p. 44

108) Gherardi, quoted from "Kellermensch in der Krise", *Der . Spiegel*, no. 48, November 21, 1966, p. 170

109) Ibid., p. 169

110) Quoted from Betti, *Fellini*, pp. 151 f.

111) See Kezich, *Fellini . . .*, p. 530

112) Tognazzi, quoted from Franco Faldini and Goffredo Fofi, *Il cinema italiano d'oggi*, Arnoldo Mondadori Editore, 1984, p. 244

113) Fellini, quoted from Betti, *Fellini*, p. 162

114) Fellini, *Aufsätze . . .*, p. 10

115) Ibid.

116) See Birgit Kraatz, "Jagd auf Fellini", *Rheinischer Merkur*, February 16, 1968

117) Fellini, quoted from Mario Devena, "Fellini! Fellini! Fellini! – Ein Gespräch", *film*, April 1968, p. 20

118) See Betti, *Fellini*, pp. 163–195

119) Fellini, quoted from Devena, "Fellini! . . .", p. 20

120) See Kezich, *Fellini . . .*, p. 547

121) Fellini, *Satyricon*, Diogenes Verlag, Zürich, 1983, p. 231

122) Fellini, quoted from Faldini and Fofi, *Il cinema italiano . . .*, p. 240

123) Fellini, *Satyricon*, p. 240

124) Ibid., pp. 235 f.

125) See Betti, *Fellini*, pp. 134 ff.

126) Fellini, quoted from Stanley Kauffmann, *Figures of Light*, Harper & Row, Publishers, 1971, p. 250

127) See Fava and Vigano, *i film . . .*, p. 41

128) See Faldini and Fofi, *Il cinema italiano . . .*, p. 242

129) Fellini, quoted from ibid.

130) Quoted from Reisfeld, "Ein meisterhafter Alptraum", p. 36

131) Fellini, *Satyricon*, p. 237

132) Fellini, quoted from Faldani and Fofi, *Il cinema italiano . . .*, p. 245

133) Fellini, quoted from his film *The Clowns*, Italy, 1970

134) Federico Fellini, "Weisser Clown und Dummer August", *Die Weltwoche*, no. 22, June 2, 1976, p. 49

135) Ibid.

136) Fellini, *Aufsätze . . .*, p. 135

137) Fellini, quoted from the press kit for *Casanova* published by 20th Century Fox, p. 15

138) Diehl, "Ich, Federico . . .", p. 108

139) Fellini, quoted from Jürgen Vordermann, "Ich möchte alle Gesichter des Planeten sehen", *Die Welt*, November 28, 1988

140) Fellini, quoted from Wiseman and Behr, "Magician of the Movies", p. 43. *Fellinis Faces* (Diogenes Verlag) can be warmly recommended to anyone who is interested in looking through Fellini's "Wanted" lists

141) Those who would like to look into the subject in more detail could begin with Horst Schäfer's *Film im Film*, Fischer Taschenbuchverlag, 1985.

142) Fellini, quoted from Pecori, *Federico Fellini*, p. 121

143) Fellini, quoted from ibid.

144) Federico Fellini, *Roma*, Diogenes Verlag, Zürich, 1972, p. 212

145) Faldini and Fofi, *Il cinema italiano . . .*, p. 247

146) Fellini, quoted from ibid., p. 248

147) Fellini, quoted from ibid.

148) Fellini, quoted from the press kit for *Amarcord*, published by Warner-Columbia Germany

149) Fellini, quoted from Grazzini, *Warum . . .*, p. 24

150) Fellini, quoted from the press kit for *Amarcord*

151) Fellini, ibid.

152) Fellini, quoted from Robert Schär, "Vom Untergang der Menschheit", *Film- und Ton-Magazin*, 12/73

153) Fellini, quoted from the press kit for *Amarcord*

154) Federico Fellini, *Amarcord*, Diogenes Verlag, Zürich, 1974, pp. 319 f.

155) Fellini, quoted from the press kit for *Casanova*, p. 2

156) Federico Fellini, *Casanova*, Diogenes Verlag, Zürich, 1977, pp. 242 f.

157) Fellini, quoted from Gian Luigi Rondi, *7 Domande a 49 registi*, Societa Editrice Internazionale, Turin, 1975, p. 227

158) "Film-Notizen", *Kölner Rundschau*, November 9, 1957

159) Fellini, quoted from Gian Luigi Rondi, *Il cinema dei maestri*, Rusconi, Milan, 1980, p. 67

160) Fellini, quoted from ibid.

161) Fellini, quoted from Georges Simenon, ". . .im Gespräch mit Federico Fellini", *Die Weltwoche*, no. 10, March 9, 1977, p. 45

162) Fellini, quoted from ibid.

163) Fellini, quoted from ibid.

164) Fellini, quoted from ibid., p. 46

165) See Fava and Vigano, *i film . . .*, p. 43

166) Pauline Kael, quoted from Kezich, *Fellini . . .*, p. 666

167) Fellini, quoted from Rondi, *Il cinema . . .*, p. 76

168) Fellini, quoted from Bachmann, "Federico Fellini", pp. 56 f.

169) Fellini, quoted from Martin Schlappner, "Mit Federico Fellini im Gespräch", *Neue Zürcher Zeitung*, June 23, 1974

170) Fellini, quoted from "Der alte Mann auf dem Meer", *Stern*, September 8, 1983, p. 75

171) Fellini, quoted from Faldini and Fofi, *Il cinema italiano . . .*, p. 258

172) See Lietta Tornabuoni, "Für mich ist selbst das Kino eine Frau", *Die Welt*, April 12, 1980, p. 18

173) The title of the LP is "Snakefinger's Vestal Virgins – Night of Desirable Objects", Red Rhino Rec., Red LP 78

174) Bo van de Graaf, "Music to the Films of Federico Fellini, Composed by Nino Rota, Played by I Compani", ITM Rec. 0026; "Amarcord Nino Rota – Interpretations of Nino Rota's Music from the Films of Federico Fellini", aris 889 301 909

175) "Chansons pour Fellini – Nino Rota/Katyna Ranieri", Milan Rec. A 329/330

176) Federico Fellini, "Eine ungewöhnliche Bekanntschaft", *Film und Fernsehen*, no. 4, 1983, p. 44

177) Fellini, quoted from Veit Mölter, "Der eine fürchtet Gott, ich fürchte das Weib", *Kölner Stadt Anzeiger*, November 8, 1980

178) Fellini, quoted from Costanzo Costantini, "Federico Fellini", *Playboy*, May, 1980, p. 72

179) Fellini, quoted from Schoonejans, *Fellinis Stadt . . .*, p. 72

180) Fellini, quoted from Costantini, "Federico Fellini", p. 72

181) See Alfred Nemeczek and Jürgen Vordemann, "Fellinis Rache an Rimini", *Stern*, March 7, 1974, p. 94

182) See Sandra Milo, *Caro Federico*, Rizzoli Editore, Milan, 1982

183) See Beatrice Schlag, "Was macht dein Hintern?", *Stern*, November 25, 1982, pp. 111

184) Fellini, quoted from the press kit for *La città delle donne*, Concorde-Film

185) Fellini, quoted from Lietta Tornabuoni, "Für mich ist selbst das Kino eine Frau", *Die Welt . . .*

186) Fellini, quoted from Costantini, "Federico Fellini", p. 74

187) Kezich, *Fellini . . .*, p. 692

188) Schlappner, *Von Rossellini . . .*, p. 250

189) Fellini, quoted from Beatrice Schlag, "Die Reise eines Mannes zu sich selbst", *Plus*, no. 28/1980, p. 12

190) Fellini, quoted from Fava and Vigano, *i film . . .*, p. 45

191) Fellini, quoted from "Und das Schiff fährt", *Film und Fernsehen*, no. 4/1984, p. 35

192) Fellini, quoted from Costantini, "Federico Fellini", p. 78

193) See Kezich, *Fellini . . .*, p. 709

194) Fellini, quoted from the press kit to *And the Ship Sails on*, Concorde-Film

195) Fellini, quoted from Kezich, *Fellini...*, pp. 713 f.

196) Ibid., p. 722

197) Federico Fellini, quoted from Pit Rieth-müller, "Filmemachen kann ich wirklich", *Süddeutsche Zeitung*, February 13, 1986

198) Fellini, quoted from the press kit for *Ginger and Fred*, Tobis Film

199) See "Personalien – Federico Fellini", *Der Spiegel*, December 7, 1987, pp. 250 f.

200) Decision quoted in Wolfgang Prosinger, "Ein erster Schlag gegen die Spot-Barbe-rei", *epd/Kirche und Rundfunk*, no. 83, October 21, 1989, p. 19

201) Fellini, quoted from ibid.

202) See "Rufschädigung?", *Frankfurter Allgemeine Zeitung*, March 8, 1986

203) See Kezich, *Fellini...*, p. 746

204) Fellini, quoted from Caen and Lacassin, *Fellini und die Comic*," p. 26

205) See Fiedler, Schlag and Sturz, *Ohne Frauen...*, p. 78

206) See Heidi Brang, "Ein Himmelsgewölbe übersät mit Sternen", *Film und Fernsehen*, 2/1989, p. 22

207) Fellini, quoted from Kraatz, "Jagd auf Fellini", *Rheinischer Merkur...*

208) Diogenes publishes Fellini's screenplays (in German)

209) Fellini, quoted from Bachmann, "Federico Fellini", pp. 58 f.

210) Fellini, quoted from Knorr and Meier, "Ich bin ein ungebildeter Mensch...", p. 37

211) Mikhalkov-Konchalovski, "Exkurs über die Wahrheit auf der Leinwand", *Filmwissenschaftliche Beiträge*, 1/1978, p. 96

212) Fellini, quoted from Johannes von Dohnanyi, "Also sprach Fellini", *Playboy*, 12/1989, p. 115

213) Fellini, quoted from Grazzini, *Warum...*, p. 113

214) Fellini, *Aufsätze...*, p. 70

215) Fellini, quoted from Birgitta Ashoff, "Warum wollen Sie nicht älter werden, Herr Fellini?", *Frankfurter Allgemeine Magazin*, June 21, 1985, p. 74

216) Fellini, quoted from the press kit for *Casanova*, p. 15

217) See Knorr and Meier, "Ich bin ein ungebildeter Mensch...", p. 37

218) Ibid.

219) Andrei Tarkovski, "Franziskaner und Gourmet", *Film und Fernsehen*, 4/1983, p. 40

220) See Tarkowski, "Die versiegelte Zeit", Ullstein 1985

221) Fellini, quoted from Pecori, *Federico Fellini*, p. 12

222) Fellini, quoted from the press kit for *The Voice of the Moon*, NEF 2 Filmverleih, Munich

223) See von Dohnanyi, "Also sprach Fellini", *Playboy...*, p. 116

224) See Danielle Heymann, "Federico Fellini: hearing voices", *Guardian Weekly*, March 4, 1990

225) Fellini, quoted from von Dohnanyi, "Also sprach Fellini", *Playboy...*, p. 114

Bibliography

Books

General Interest – Interviews – Portraits –
Regarding Individual Films

Aiello, Gianni – *Il cinema italiano negli ultimi vent'anni*, Gianni Manglarotti Editore, Cremona, *no date*

Aspekte des italienischen Films I, Verband der deutschen Filmclubs e. V. (ed.), brochure of the Bad Ems Film Festival, April 30–May 4, 1969

Bachmann, Gideon – "Federico Fellini", in: Gragor, Ulrich (ed.); *Wie sie filmen*, Sigbert Mohn Verlag, Gütersloh, 1966 pp. 54–78

Bawden, Liz-Anne (ed.) – *rororo Filmlexikon*, Rowohlt Taschenbuch Verlag, Hamburg 1978, Vol. IV, p. 960 f.

Bellone, Julius (ed.) – *Renaissance of the Film*, Collier-Macmillan Ltd., London 1970, pp. 79–90, 264–276

Betti, Liliana – *Fellini*, Diogenes Verlag, Zurich 1980

Betti, Liliana and Angelucci, Gianfranco – *Casanova rendez-vous con Federico Fellini*, Bompiani, Milan 1975

Boyer, Deena – *Die 200 Tage von 8½*, Rowohlt Taschenbuch Verlag, Hamburg 1963

Canziani, Alfonso – *Gli anni del neorealismo*, La Nuova Italia Editrice, Florence 1977

Codelli, Lorenzo – "Ginger e Fred," in: Cowie, Peter (ed.) – *Film Guide 1987*, The Tantivy Press, New York p. 223 f.

Cosulich, Callisto – *I film dei Alberto Lattuada*, Gremese Editrice, Rome 1985

Faldini, Franca and Fofi, Goffredo – *Il Cinema Italiano d'Oggi*, 1970 – 1984. Arnoldo Mondatori Editore, 1984

Fava, Claudio G. and Viganò, Aldo – *I film di Federico Fellini*, Gremese Editore, Rome 1987

Fellini, Federico – *Achteinhalb*, Diogenes Verlag, Zurich 1974

Fellini, Federico – *Amarcord*, Diogenes Verlag, Zurich 1974

Fellini, Federico – *Aufsätze und Notizen*, Diogenes Verlag, Zurich 1981

Fellini, Federico – *Casanova*, Diogenes Verlag, Zurich 1977

Fellini, Federico – *E la nave va*, Diogenes Verlag, Zurich 1984

Fellini, Federico – *Ginger und Fred*, Diogenes Verlag, Zurich 1986

Fellini, Federico – *Intervista*, Diogenes Verlag, Zurich 1987

Fellini, Federico – *Julia und die Geister*, Diogenes Verlag, Zurich 1965

Fellini, Federico – *La dolce vita*, Diogenes Verlag, Zurich 1974

Fellini, Federico – *La strada*, Diogenes Verlag, Zurich 1977

Fellini, Federico – *Le notti di Cabiria*, Garzanti Editore, Milan 1981

Fellini, Federico – *Lo sciecco bianco*, Garzanti Editore, Milan 1980

Fellini, Federico – *Die Müßiggänger*, Diogenes Verlag, Zurich 1977

Fellini, Federico – *Die Nächte der Cabiria*, Diogenes Verlag, Zurich 1977

Fellini, Federico – *Orchesterprobe*, Diogenes Verlag, Zurich 1979

Fellini, Federico – *Roma*, Diogenes Verlag, Zurich 1972

Fellini, Federico – *Satyricon*, Diogenes Verlag, Zurich 1983

Fellini, Federico – *Stadt der Frauen*, Diogenes Verlag, Zurich 1980

Fellini, Federico – "The Bitter Life – of Money," in: Geduld, Harry M. (ed.) – *Film Makers on Film Making*, Indiana University Press 1967, pp. 191–194

Fellini, Federico – *Un Regista a Cinecittà*, Arnoldo Mondadori Editore, Milan 1988

Der Film in Europa, Dokumente Verlag, Offenburg in Baden 1955, pp. 57–63

Filmlexicon degli autori e delle opere, Edizione di Bianco e Nero, Rome 1959, pp. 646–649

Fischer Film Almanach, Fischer Taschenbuch Verlag, Frankfurt am Main, Vol. 1981, p. 165 f.; Vol. 1984, p. 61; Vol. 1985, p. 62 f.

Fischer, Robert – "Fellinis Stadt der Frauen," in: Just, Lothar (ed.) – *Filmjahr 1980/81*, Filmland Presse, Munich 1981, p. 81

Grazzini, Giovanni – *Gli Anni Sessanta In Cento Film*, Editore Laterza, Rome 1977, pp. 35–40, 142–147, 243–246, 296–301

Grazzini, Giovanni – *Warum machen Sie nicht mal eine schöne Liebesgeschichte?* Diogenes Verlag, Zurich 1984

Gregor, Ulrich and Patalas, Enno – *Geschichte des Films*, C. Bertelsmann Verlag, Gütersloh 1973, pp. 321–345

Hall, Calvin S. and Lindzey, Gardner – *Theorien der Persönlichkeit*, Vol. I, Verlag C. H. Beck, Munich 1978, pp. 98–136

Handbuch der Katholischen Filmkritik, Verlag Haus Altenberg, Düsseldorf, Vol. V, pp. 206, 250, 318, 469 f.; Vol. VI, pp. 106, 166; Vol. VII, pp. 10, 24, 25; Vol. VIII, pp. 86, 158; Vol. IX, pp. 15, 54, 88; Vol. X, pp. 82, 268; Vol. XI, pp. 107, 274

Hanisch, Michael – "Erinnerung und Phantasie," in: Knietzsch, Horst (ed.) *Prisma, Kino- und Fernseh-Almanach Nr. 16*, Henschelverlag Kunst und Gesellschaft, Berlin 1985, pp. 201–214

Hoffmann, Hilmar and Schobert, Walter (ed.) – *Fellini: Zeichnungen-, Schriftenreihe des Deutschen Filmmuseums*, Frankfurt am Main 1984

Jansen, Peter W. and Schütte, Wolfram (ed.) – *Roberto Rosselini – Reihe Film 36*, Carl Hanser Verlag, Munich 1987

Kael, Pauline – *Kiss Kiss Bang Bang*, Atlantic Monthly Press Book, Boston, Toronto 1968, pp. 318, 351 f., 365 f., 368

Kalbus, Oskar – *Filme der Gegenwart*, Ewalt Skulima Verlag, Heidelberg 1957, pp. 363–368

Kauffmann, Stanley – *Figures of Light*, Harper & Row, New York, Evanston, San Francisco, London 1971, pp. 196–254

Kezich, Tullio – *Fellini – Eine Biographie*, Diogenes Verlag, Zurich 1989

Krusche, Dieter – *Reclams Film Führer*, Philipp Reclam, Jr., Stuttgart 1982, pp. 32, 82, 161 f., 186, 381 f., 399 f., 500 f., 568

Lyon, Christopher (ed.) – *Directors/Film-makers*, Macmillan Publishers, London 1984, pp. 171–175

Metz, Christian – *Semiologie des Films*, Wilhelm Fink Verlag, Munich 1972, pp. 289–297

Michael, Paul – *The Academy Awards: A Pictorial History*, Crown Publishers, Inc., New York, Updated Fifth Edition 1982

Michalkow-Kontschalowski, Andrej – "Exkurs über die Wahrheit auf der Leinwand," in: *Filmwissenschaftliche Beiträge*, published by the *Hochschule für Film und Fernsehen der DDR*, Nr. 1/1978, pp. 84–120

Pecori, Franci – *Federico Fellini*, La Nuova Italia Editrice, Florence 1978

Rondi, Gian-Luigi – *Il Cinema dei Maestri*, Rusconi, Milan 1980, pp. 67–90

Rondi, Gian-Luigi; Crowther, Bosley and Sacchi, Filippo – *Italian Cinema Today*, Carlo Bestetti, Edizione d'Arte 1966, pp. 92–111

Rondi, Gian-Luigi – *7 domande a 49 registi*, Socistà Editrice Internazionale, Turin 1975, pp. 227–235

Schäfer, Horst – *Film im Film*, Fischer Taschenbuch Verlag, Frankfurt am Main 1985, pp. 85–117

Scheugl, Hans and Schmidt, Jr., Ernst – *Lexicon des Avantgarde-, Experimental- und Undergroundfilms*, Vol. I, Suhrkamp Verlag 1974, pp. 378–383, 950–953

Schlappner, Martin – *Von Rossellini bis Fellini*, Origo, Zurich 1958

Schoonejans, Sonja – *Fellinis Stadt der Frauen*, Wilhelm Heyne Verlag, Munich 1980

Siciliano, Enzo – *Pasolini – Leben und Werk*, Beltz & Gelberg, Weinheim 1980

Stresau, Norbert – *Der Oscar*, Wilhelm Heyne Verlag, Munich 1985

Tarkowski, Andrei – *Die versiegelte Zeit*, Ullstein 1985

Thomson, David – *A Biographical Dictionary of the Cinema*, Secker & Warburg, London 1975, pp. 166–168

Toeplitz, Jerzy – *Geschichte des Films*, Vol. I, pp. 61–68, 473–506; Vol. II, pp. 1579–1605

Winter, Mona – "Ein unermüdlicher Sucher: Fellinis Ikonographie der Sinnlichkeiten," in: *Lust und Elend: Das erotische Kino*, Verlag C. J. Bucher, Munich and Lucerne 1981, pp. 94–113

Articles

General Interest – Interviews – Portraits

Ashoff, Birgitta – "Warum wollen Sie nicht älter werden, Herr Fellini?" in: *Frankfurter Allgemeine Magazin*, June 21, 1985, p. 74 f.

Bachmann, Gideon – "Gespräch mit Federico Fellini," in: *film*, Oct./Nov. 1964, pp. 5–9

Baer, Volker – "Ein Mikrokosmos der römischen Welt," in: *Der Tagesspiegel*, Jan. 14, 1990

Berghoff, Gert – "Film ist mein Leben geworden," in: *Kölnische Rundschau*, Feb. 17, 1986

Berghoff, Gert – "Spiegelbilder der Sehnsüchte," in: *Kölnische Rundschau*, Jan. 18, 1985

Bienik, Martin – "Panoptikum der Phallust," in: *die tageszeitung*, Aug. 25, 1984

Brang, Heidi – "Ein Himmelsgewölbe, übersät mit Sternen," in: *Film und Fernsehen* No. 2/ 1989, pp. 20–22

"Britische Eröffnung, sonst alles im Zeichen von Fellini," in: *Blickpunkt: Film*, March 25, 1988, p. 20 f.

Burkamp, Gisela – "Die Groteske eskaliert zum Psycho-Comic," in: *Neue Westfälische*, Aug. 11, 1964

Caen, Michael and Lacassin, Francis – "Fellini und die Comics," in: *film*, Feb. 1965, p. 24 ff.

Campesi, Vernon – "Ein Mann zog aus, um den Zirkus des Lebens filmisch zu bewältigen," in: *Der Mittag*, Jan. 11, 1964

"Cinecittà – ein fünfzigjähriger Traum," in: *Neue Zürcher Zeitung*, April 30, 1987

"Clip-Kunst: 'Ganz Bayern in einem Bier,'" in: *Der Spiegel*, July 20, 1987, p. 136 f.

Constantini, Costanzo – "Federico Fellini," in: *Playboy*, May 1981, pp. 67–78

Davis, Melton S. – "Filmemacher Federico Fellini," in: *Das Beste*, Aug. 8, 1972, pp. 48–53

Devena, Marlo – "Fellini! Fellini! Fellini! Ein Gespräch," in: *film*, April 1968, p. 19 f.

Diehl, Ute – "Ich, Federico, Kaiser und Clown," in: *Westermanns Monatshefte*, March 1973, pp. 42–49, 108

von Dohnanyi, Johannes – "Also sprach Fellini," in: *Playboy*, Dec. 1989, pp. 110–116

Draeger, Wolfhart – "Fellini und seine Geister," in: *Die Welt*, Dec. 5, 1989

Feldman, Sebastian – "Der große Circusdirektor," in: *Rheinische Post*, Jan. 18, 1990

Fellini, Federico – "Eine ungewöhnliche Bekanntschaft," in: *Film und Fernsehen*, No. 4/ 1983, p. 43 f.

Fellini, Federico – "Ich bin ein Lügner, aber ein aufrichtiger," in: *Deutsche Zeitung*, June 21, 1974, p. 23

Fellini, Federico – "Weißer Clown und dummer August," in: *Die Weltwoche*, June 2, 1976, p. 49

"Fellinis intimes Gespräch," in: *Neue Zürcher Zeitung*, July 18, 1985

Fiedler, Teja; Schlag, Beatrice; Sturz, Gerlad – "Ohne Frauen gibt es keinen Zauber," in: *Stern*, Nov. 5, 1987

Fofi, Goffredo – "Lachen auf Italienisch," in: *Filmkritik*, No. 8/1964, pp. 396–402

Galle, Mische – "Die Wahrheit des Menschen," in: *Neue Rhein Zeitung*, Feb. 28, 1965

Gallus, Rudolf and Berghahn, Wilfried – "Fragen an Cesare Zavatinni," in: *Filmkritik*, No. 2/ 1962, pp. 51–56

Gehler, Fred – "Das einzige Spiel," in: *Film und Fernsehen*, No. 4/1983, p. 41

"Ein gewisses Lächeln," in: *Der Spiegel*, Feb. 26, 1958, p. 46 ff.

"Der Giuseppe Verdi des Film-Italiens, Fellini, 50 Jahre," in: *Westfälische Allgemeine Zeitung*, Jan. 20, 1970

Görner, Eberhard – "Fremder in der Nacht: Fellinis Zeichnungen," in: *Film und Fernsehen*, No. 2/1989, p. 32 f.

Graf Schwerin, Christoph – "Giuliettas Clowngesicht," in: *Die Welt*, Aug. 11, 1984

Hermann, Jörg – "Wir gehen auf den Tod des Kinos zu," in: *medium*, No. 10/1984, p. 24 ff.

"Ich bin ein Lügner, aber ein aufrichtiger," in: *die Tageszeitung*, Aug. 31, 1985, p. 13

Jeremias, Brigitte – "Die Vision ist die Realität," in: *Frankfurter Allgemeine Zeitung*, Dec. 31, 1976

Jessen, Jens – "Gespensterjagd," in: *Frankfurter Allgemeine Zeitung*, Oct. 10, 1989

Jurczyk, Günter – "Selbst Celentano zieht nicht mehr," in: *Kölner Stadt-Anzeiger*, Aug. 17, 1985

Jurczyk, Günter – "Federico Fellinis Studio in Rom ist verweist," in: *Der Tagesspiegel*, Sept. 3, 1989

"Kellermensch in der Krise," in: *Der Spiegel*, Nov. 21, 1966, p. 169 f.

Kilb, Andreas – "Asa nisi masa," in: *Die Zeit*, Jan. 19, 1990

Klüver, Henning – "Als klein Caesar groß raus kam," in: *Zeitmagazin*, May 18, 1984

Knorr, Wolfgang and Meier, Marco – "Ich bin ein ungebildeter Mensch und mache Filme," in: *Die Weltwoche*, Jan. 26, 1984, p. 37

Kraatz, Birgit – "Jagd auf Fellini," in: *Rheinischer Merkur*, Feb. 16, 1968

Ladiges, Peter M. – "Fellini, il poeta und das Horn des Stiers," in: *Filmkritik*, No. 8/1967, pp. 463–467

Lahann, Birgit – "Die tausend Gesichter des Fellini," in: *Stern*, April 2, 1981, p. 112 ff.

Lehmann, Hans – "Magier in Cinecittà," in: *Rheinische Post*, Jan. 19, 1985

"Menschlichkeit, Alpträume und Satire," in: *Neue Zürcher Zeitung*, Jan. 17, 1980

Prosinger, Wolfgang – "Ein erster Schlag gegen die Spot-Barbarei," in: *epd/Kirche und Rundfunk*, Oct. 21, 1989, p. 19

Rhode, Eric – "Fellini's Double City," in: *Encounter*, June 1964, pp. 44–49

Riethmüller, Pit and Spagnoletti, Giovanni – "Kunst ohne Mut und Kraft," in: *Süddeutsche Zeitung*, Nov. 24/25, 1984, p. 136

Schlag, Beatrice – "Was macht dein Hintern?" in: *Stern*, Nov. 25, 1982, p. 111 f.

Schlappner, Martin – "Mit Federico Fellini im Gespräch," in: *Neue Zürcher Zeitung*, June 23, 1974

Schlitter, Horst – "Italiens Fernsehen darf Filme nicht mit Werbung unterbrechen," in: *Frankfurter Rundschau*, Oct. 18, 1989

Seeßlen, Georg – "Cesare Zavattini," in: *epd Film*, No. 1/1990, p. 10

Seeßlen, Georg – "Sechs Arten, Fellini zu verehren," in: *epd Film*, p. 24–29

Tarkowski, Andrei – "Franziskaner und Gourmet," in: *Film und Fernsehen*, No. 4/1983, pp. 39–44

Ungeheuer, Barbara – "Der berühmte Regisseur," in: *Brigitte*, Aug. 10, 1978, p. 124 ff.

"Die vier Karrieren des Federico Fellini," in: *Film & Ton Magazin*, Feb. 1, 1973, p. 30 f.

"Der Visionär als der einzig wahre Realist," in: *Neue Zürcher Zeitung*, Dec. 9, 1976

Vordemann, Jürgen – "Ich möchte alle Gesichter des Planeten sehen," in: *Die Welt*, Nov. 28, 1988

Vordemann, Jürgen – "Die Melancholie des Zirkusdirektors," in: *Die Welt*, Jan. 19, 1990

Walter, Eugene – "Meister der Widersprüche," in: *Der Monat*, Dec. 1965, pp. 57–67

"Wege zum Ich und darüber hinaus," in: *Neue Zürcher Zeitung*, Jan. 18, 1990

Wiegand, Wilfried – "Federico Fellini," in: *Frankfurter Allgemeine Magazin*, June 15, 1984

Wiegand, Wilfried – "Fellini und die Frauen," in: *Frankfurter Allgemeine Magazin*, July 4, 1980, p. 24 f.

Wiegand, Wilfried – "Italien ist überall," in: *Frankfurter Allgemeine Magazin*, Jan. 19, 1980

Willschrei, Karl H. – "Eifriger Müßiggänger der Filmkunst," in: *Neue Rhein Zeitung*, Dec. 1, 1962

Wilmes, Hartmut – "Er entfesselt die Bilderstürme," in: *Kölnische Rundschau*, Jan. 19, 1990

Wiseman, Carter S. and Behr, Edward – "Magician of the Movies," in: *Newsweek*, Aug. 18, 1975, p. 40 f.

Zellweger, Harry – "Magier des italienischen Films," in: *Stuttgarter Zeitung*, Jan. 22, 1985

Zimmermann, Gernot W. – "Eine lebende Legende auf Reisen," in: *Die Presse*, March 15, 1988, p. 14

Zimmermann, Gernot W. – "Sich ununterbrochen schamlos erzählen," in: *Die Presse*, March 19/20, 1988, p. 7

Regarding Individual Films

La Strada:
Korn, Karl – "La Strada, das Wunder eines Films," in: *Frankfurter Allgemeine Zeitung*, Sept. 17, 1956

The Swindle:
"Il Bidone," in: *Der Spiegel*, Sept. 11, 1957;
"Der Kardinal von Köpenick," in: *Der Spiegel*, Nov. 16, 1955;
Kotulla, Theodor – "Il Bidone," in: *Filmkritik*, No. 10/1957, p. 147 f.

The Nights of Cabiria:
"Die Nächte der Cabiria," in: *Der Spiegel*, Oct. 23, 1957;
Mogge, Wilhelm – "Die Nächte der Cabiria," in: *Kölnische Rundschau*, Dec. 14, 1957

La Dolce Vita:
Brenner, Wolfgang – "Rom, sündige Stadt," in: *tip*, Jan. 23, 1986, p. 50 f.;
Schütte, Wolfram – "Leben mit ausgebliebenen Erwartungen," in: *Frankfurter Rundschau*, April 4, 1986;
"Das süße Leben," in: *Der Spiegel*, Feb. 17, 1960

The Temptation of Dr. Antonio:
"Boccacio '70," in: *Filmkritik*, No. 9/1962, p. 427 f.

8½:
"8½," in: *Filmkritik*, No. 7/1963, pp. 326–330;
"Asa Nisi Masa," in: *Der Spiegel*, Nov. 28, 1962;
"Eine Art von Testament," in: *Neue Rhein Zeitung*, Aug. 5, 1963;
"Fellini 8½," in: *film*, No. 1/1963;
Ladiges, Peter M. – "8½," in: *film*, No. 3/1963, p. 34 f.

Juliet of the Spirits:
"Drang zur Droge," in: *Der Spiegel*, Sept. 5, 1966;
Färber, Helmut – "Julia und die Geister," in: *Filmkritik*, No. 11/1965, p. 687 ff.;
"Julchen und die Geister," in: *Der Spiegel*, March 10, 1965;
"Julia und die Geister," in: *Der Spiegel*, Nov. 24, 1965, p. 169;
Wendt, Ernst – "Julia und die Beatles," in: *film*, No. 12/1965, pp. 10–15

Fellini's Satyricon:
"Athleten vom Schlachthof," in: *Der Spiegel*, Sept. 30, 1968, p. 186;
Halstenberg, Armin – "Ich bin kein Messias," in: *Kölner Stadt-Anzeiger*, March 7, 1970;
"Kannibalen am Lido," in: *Der Spiegel*, Sept. 15, 1969, p. 188;
Reisfeld, Bert – "Ein Meisterhafter Alptraum," in: *Stuttgarter Zeitung*, Jan. 23, 1970;
"Satyricon," in: *Filmkritik*, No. 3/1970, p. 157

The Clowns:
Reichold, Hermann – "Die Clowns," in: *Filmbeobachter*, No. 5, March 1982, p. 6

Roma:
"Wie man ißt," in: *Der Spiegel*, Nov., 1972, p. 172

Amarcord:
Bondy, François – "Macht des Schattens," in: *Die Weltwoche*, Dec. 1973;
Ferber, Christian – "Fellinis Rimini, die Welt, in der wir leben," in: *Die Welt*, March 11, 1974;
Halstenberg, Armin – "Weltuntergang in der Provinz," in: *Kölner Stadt-Anzeiger*, May 25/26, 1974;
Nemeczek, Alfred and Vordermann, Jürgen – "Fellinis Rache an Rimini," in: *Stern*, March 7, 1974, p. 90 ff.;
Schär, Robert – "Vom Untergang der Menschheit," in: *Film- und Ton-Magazin*, No. 12/1973;
Schober, Siegfried – "Ich will eine Frau," in: *Der Spiegel*, April 1, 1974

Fellini's Casanova:
Bachman, Gideon – "Ein Mann baut seine Welt," in: *Die Weltwoche*, March 9, 1977;
Blumenberg, Hans C. – "Cazzomàs auf dem Planet der Frauen," in: *Die Zeit*, Feb. 25, 1977;
"Ein Pinoccio, der niemals Mensch wird," in: *Neue Zürcher Zeitung*, March 17, 1977;
Kessler, Sinah – "Casanova, keuchend, komisch, keusch," in: *Frankfurter Allgemeine Zeitung*, Dec. 15, 1976;
Mölter, Veit – "Die Ehrlichkeit von Casanova," in: *Kölner Stadt-Anzeiger*, July 21, 1976;
Mölter, Veit – "Heidnischer Bilderbogen mit Casanovas Tatenruhm," in: *Neue Rhein Zeitung*, June 20, 1976;
Nemeczek, Alfred – "Fellinis Masken, Orgien und Legenden," in: *Stern*, March 31, 1977;
Petz, Thomas – "Das große, schöne Welt-Abräumung," in: *Süddeutsche Zeitung*, Dec. 15, 1976;
Petz, Thomas – "Märtyrer seiner Triebe," in: *Die Weltwoche*, Dec. 22, 1976;
Schär, Robert – "Sympathie für einen Verrückten," in: *Der Tagesspiegel*, March 20, 1977;
Schober, Siegfried – "Ein Gefangener des Sexus," in: *Der Spiegel*, Dec. 6, 1976, p. 209 ff.;
Simenon, Georges – ". . . im Gespräch mit Federico Fellini," in: *Die Weltwoche*, March 9, 1977, p. 45 f.;
Widmer, Urs – "Casanova war nur ein Angeber," in: *Stern*, June 24, 1976, p. 112 ff.;
Wiegand, Wilfried – "Ein Profi der Lüste," in: *Frankfurter Allgemeine Zeitung*, Feb. 28, 1977

Orchestra Rehearsal:
Baas, Balduin – "Fellini ist eine Zeige," in: *Playboy*, Oct. 1979, p. 18;
"Chaos voller Geigen," in: *Der Spiegel*, Feb. 12, 1979, p. 177 f.;
Kötz, Michael – "Kakaphonische Harmonie," in: *Frankfurter Rundschau*, June 7, 1983;
Limmer, Wolfgang – "Magier im geplanten Chaos," in: *Der Spiegel*, June 12, 1978, p. 214 f.;
Schmidt, Dietmar – "Ein ganz anderer Fellini," in: *Stuttgarter Zeitung*, April 20, 1979

La Città delle Donne:
Bachmann, Gideon – "Fellinis Abschied vom Gockel," in: *Stern*, Aug. 2, 1979, p. 32 ff.;
"Barocker Ego-Trip in Talmi und Puder," in: *Der Spiegel*, July 30, 1979, p. 132 ff.;
Groh, Christopher – "Federico Fellinis letzter wundersamer Traum," in: *Neue Zürcher Zeitung*, Feb. 7, 1980;
"Ich glaube, das Kino ist eine Frau," in: *Stern*, Oct. 23, 1980, p. 270 ff.;
Mölter, Veit – "Der eine fürchtet Gott, ich fürchte das Weib," in: *Kölner Stadt-Anzeiger*, Nov. 8, 1980;
Mölter, Veit – "Federico Fellinis Furcht vorm Weib," in: *Westfälische Rundschau*, Nov. 8, 1980;
Schlag, Beatrice – "Die Reise eines Mannes zu sich selbst," in: *Plus*, No. 28/1980, p. 10 ff.;
Tornabuoni, Lietta – "Für mich ist selbst das Kino eine Frau," in: *Die Welt*, April 12, 1980;
"Traumreise in die (männliche) Seele," in: *Neue Zürcher Zeitung*, May 29, 1980;
Witte, Karsten – "Ein Mann auf der Rutschbahn," in: *Die Zeit*, Oct. 31, 1980

And the Ship Sails On:
Fründt, Bodo – "Bilder gegen die Vergeblichkeit," in: *Süddeutsche Zeitung*, Oct. 12, 1984;
Jenny Urs – "Das Abendland in einem Boot," in: *Der Spiegel*, Oct. 15, 1984, p. 236 f.;
Künzel, Uwe – "Fellinis Schiff der Träume," in: *epd Film*, No. 10/1984, p. 23;
Löffler, Sigrid – "Untergang der Belcanto 'Titanic,'" in: *profil*, Oct. 15, 1984, p. 75 ff.;
Lutterbeck, Claus – "Der alte Mann und das Meer," in: *Stern*, Sept. 8, 1983, p. 70 f.;
"Das Melodrama einer Kreuzfahrt in die Katastrophe," in: *Neue Zürcher Zeitung*, Jan. 26, 1984;
Mölter, Veit – "Feuerwerk zum Tod des Kinos," in: *Kölner Stadt-Anzeiger*, March 25, 1983;
Schmidt, Georg – "Luxusliner Potemkin," in: *tip*, Oct. 19, 1984, p. 37 ff.;
Schober, Siegfried – "Große Oper, Kleine Wirkung," in: *Die Zeit*, Oct. 12, 1984;
Schütte, Wolfram – "Und das Kino läuft aus," in: *Frankfurter Rundschau*, Nov. 3, 1984;
Seidel, Hans-Dieter – "Der Dampfer als Nußschale," in: *Frankfurter Allgemeine Zeitung*, Oct. 25, 1984;
"Und das Schiff fährt," in: *Film und Fernsehen*, No. 4/1984, p. 35 f.

Ginger and Fred:
"Breitseite gegen den Bildschirm," in: *Stern*, Feb. 20, 1986, p. 174 ff.;
Görich, Knut – "Zwanzigeinhalb im Bahnhof von Rom," in: *Rheinischer Merkur/Christ und die Welt*, April 20, 1985;
Kerr, Charlotte – "Fellini dreht," in: *Indiskret*, No. 1/1986, p. 78 ff.;
Lacayo, Richard – "A World Going Down the Tube," in: *Time*, Jan. 27, 1986, p. 30 f.;
Ledel, Michael – "Ginger und Fred," in: *Film-Faust*, No. 52/1986, p. 25 ff.;
Reim, Regine – "Hollywood tanzt," in: *Frankfurter Rundschau*, March 28, 1985;
Riethmüller, Pit – "Filmemachen kann ich wirklich," in: *Süddeutsche Zeitung*, Feb. 13, 1986;
Seidel, Hans-Dieter – "Der Künstler als alter Narr," in: *Frankfurter Allgemeine Zeitung*, Feb. 15, 1986;

Seidl, Claudius – "Wenn Neil Postman zweimal klingelt," in: *Süddeutsche Zeitung*, April 25, 1986;
"Rufschädigung?" in: *Frankfurter Allgemeine Zeitung*, March 8, 1986;
"Die Traumtänzer," in: *Der Spiegel*, Feb. 17, 1986, p. 206 ff.

Intervista:
Blum, Doris – "Und dann und wann ein dicker Elefant," in: *Die Welt*, Nov. 9, 1987;
Eue, Ralph – "Stadt der Träume," in: *tip*, Nov. 12, 1987, p. 46 ff.;
Fiedler, Teja; Schlag, Beatrice und Sturz, Gerald – "Ohne Frauen gibt es keinen Zauber," in: *Stern*, Nov. 5, 1987, p. 76 ff.;
Fink, Hans-Jürgen – "Die Meute treibt den Magier in die Enge," in: *Rheinischer Merkur*, Oct. 30, 1987;
"Garantiert Plastik," in: *die tageszeitung*, Nov. 12, 1987;
Haase, Marlis – "Tränen kullern in den Grappa," in: *Neue Rhein Zeitung*, Nov. 13, 1987;
"Huldigung an das Kino als Freiheit des Spiels," in: *Neue Zürcher Zeitung*, Aug. 27, 1987;
Kilb, Andreas – "Lauter kleine Reisen in die Hölle," in: *Die Zeit*, Nov. 13, 1987, p. 59 f.;
Kreimeler, Klaus – "Das Chaos hinter der Kamera," in: *Frankfurter Rundschau*, Nov. 12, 1987;
Schmitt, Sigrid – "Federico Fellinis Intervista," in: *filmecho*, Nov. 28, 1987, p. 14 f.;
Seidl, Claudius – "Eingetragenes Markenzeichen, ges. geschützt," in: *Süddeutsche Zeitung*, Nov. 16, 1987;
Stempel, Hans – "Federico Fellinis Intervista," in: *epd Film*, No. 11/1987, p. 36

La Voce della Luna:
Buchka, Peter – "Fellinis Endspiel," in: *Süddeutsche Zeitung*, May 31, 1990;
Heymann, Daniele – "Federico Fellini: hearing voices," in: *Guardian Weekly*, March 4, 1990;
Lueken, Verena – "Spiegeltanz in Fellinis Namen," in: *Frankfurter Allgemeine Zeitung*, May 31, 1990;
Messias, Hans – "Die Poesie des Alltags," in: *Film-Korrespondenz*, May 25, 1990;
Tornabene, Francesco – "Poesie in Chaos," in: *De Schnüss*, June 1990, p. 114

Discography

Nicola Piovani, *Federico Fellini's Intervista*. Original soundtrack. Virgin Rec. 208.760-630

Nicola Piovani, *Ginger e Fred*. Original soundtrack. aris 883.266.919

Gianfranco Plenizio, *E la nave va*. Original soundtrack. aris 880.382.919

Nino Rota, *Fellini/Rota*. Original title music from various Fellini films. Silva Screen sales department of Colloseum Records, Nuremberg

Nino Rota, *Fellini/Rota – Il Bidone, Juliette des Esprits*. Original soundtrack. Corona CAM 500.001

Nino Rota, *Concerto di Misiche da Film*. Original title music from various Fellini films. aris 806.396

Nino Rota, *Music to Films of Fellini*. New arrangements of Nino Rota compositions by Ba van de Graaf. ITM Rec. 0.026

Nino Rota/Katyna Rainiere, *Chansons Pour Fellini*. aris 807.227

Nino Rota, *Amarcord Nino Rota*. Nino Rota compositions interpreted by Carla Bley, Dave Samuels, Bill Frisell, et al.

Nino Rota, *La Strada*. Original music from the ballet of the same name. EMI Italiana 2.704.021

Filmography

Variety Lights

Original title . . . . Luci del varietà
Year of origin 1950
Production company . . Capitolium Film Rome,
. . . . under the financial participation
. . . . of the cast and crew
Executive producer . . . . Bianca Lattuada
Running time . . . . approx. 100 Min.
First showing in Italy 1950

Production

Director . . . . Federico Fellini
Idea . . . . Federico Fellini
Screenplay . . . Federico Fellini, Ennio Flaiano,
. . . . Alberto Lattuada, Tullio Pinelli
Photographic direction . . . . . Otello Martelli
Camera . . . . Luciano Trasatti
Editing . . . . Mario Bonotti
Music . . . . Felice Lattuada
Scenery . . . . Aldo Buzzi
Costumes . . . . Aldo Buzzi

Cast

Role	Actor
Checco Dalmonte	Peppino De Filippo
Melina Amour	Giulietta Masina
Liliana	Carla Del Poggio
Renzo	Carlo Romano
Valeria	Gina Mascetti
Adelmo Conti	Folco Lulli
Johnny	John Kitzmiller
Bruno Antonini	Silvio Bagolini
Remo	Dante Maggio
Choreographer	Franca Valeri
The Fakir	Giulio Calí
	and many others

The White Sheik

Original title . . . . Lo sceicco bianco
Year of origin 1952
Production company . . . . P.D.C./O.F.I. Rome
Producer . . . . Luigi Rovere
Executive producer . . . . . . Enzo Provenzale
Format . . . . 35 mm, black and white/normal
Running time . . . . approx. 85 Min.
First showing in Italy . . . . Sept. 6, 1952

Production

Director . . . . Federico Fellini
Idea . . . . Michelangelo Antonioni,
. . . . Federico Fellini, Tullio Pinelli
Screenplay . . . Federico Fellini, Ennio Flaiano,
. . . . Tullio Pinelli
Photographic direction . . . . . . Arturo Gallea
Camera . . . . Antonio Belviso
Editing . . . . Rolando Benedetti
Music . . . . Nino Rota
Scenery . . . . Raffaelo Rolfo
Sound . . Armando Grilli, Walfredo Traversari

Cast

Role	Actor
Wanda Giardino Cavalli	Brunella Bovo
Ivan Cavalli	Leopoldo Trieste

Fernando Rivoli, The White Sheik	
	Alberto Sordi
Cabiria	Giulietta Masina
Felga	Lilia Landi
Director of the picture novel	Ernesto Almirante
Marilena Verlardi	Fanny Marchiò
Fernando's wife	Gina Mascetti
Ivan's uncle	Ettore Margadonna
Hotel porter	Enzio Maggio
	and many others

The Young and the Passionate

Original title . . . . I vitelloni
Year of origin 1953
Production companies . . . . . Peg Film Rome,
. . . . Citè Film Paris
Producer . . . . Lorenzo Pegoraro
Executive producer . . . . Luigi Ciacosi
Format . . . . 35 mm, black and white/normal
Running time . . . . approx. 103 Min.
First showing in Italy . . . . . . Aug. 26, 1953
Awards (among others): Nastro d'argento for Best
Film, Best Director, and Best Supporting Actor

Production

Director . . . . Federico Fellini
Idea . . . . . . Federico Fellini, Tullio Pinelli,
. . . . Ennio Flaiano
Screenplay . . . Federico Fellini, Ennio Flaiano
Photographic direction . . . . Otello Martelli,
. . . . Luciano Trasati
Camera . . . . Roberto Girardi, Franco Villa
Editing . . . . Rolando Benedetti
Music . . . . Nino Rota
Scenery . . . . Mario Chiari
Costumes . . . . M. Marinari Bomarzi

Cast

Role	Actor
Moraldo	Franco Interlenghi
Alberto	Alberto Sordi
Leopoldo	Leopoldo Trieste
Riccardo	Riccardo Fellini
Fausto	Franco Fabrizzi
Sandra	Leonora Ruffo
Fausto's father	Jean Brochard
Alberto's sister	Claude Farell
Fausto's chef	Carlo Romano
The chef's wife	Lida Baarova
Sandra's father	Enrico Viarisio
Sandra's mother	Paola Borboni
The old actor	Achille Majeroni
The unknown person in the cinema	Arlette Sauvage
The idiot	Silvio Bagolini
	and many others

Una Agenzia Matrimoniale

Original title . . . . . Un'agenzia matrimoniale
Fourth episode from . . . . . . Love in the City
(Directors of the other episodes:
. . . . Carlo Lizzani,
. . . . Michelangelo Antonioni, Dino Risi,
. . . . Francesco Maselli and Cesare
. . . . Zavattini, Alberto Lattuada)
Year of origin 1953
Production company . . . . Faro Film

Producers . . . . Cesare Zavattini,
. . . . Renato Ghione, Marco Ferreri
Executive producer . . . . . . Cesare Zavattini
Format . . . . 35 mm, black and white/normal
Length of episode . . . . approx. 23 Min.
First showing in Italy . . . . Nov. 1953

Production

Director . . . . Federico Fellini
Idea . . . . Federico Fellini
Screenplay . . . . Federico Fellini, Tullio Pinelli
Photographic direction . . . Gianni Di Venazano
Editing . . . . Eraldo Da Roma
Music . . . . Mario Nascimbene
Scenery . . . . Gianni Polidori

Cast

Role	Actor
The Journalist	Antonio Cifariello

as well as acting students from CENTRO
SPERIMENTALE DI CINEMATOGRAFÍA in
Rome

La Strada

Original title . . . . La strada
Year of origin 1954
Producers . . . . Carlo Ponti, Dino De Laurentiis
Executive producer . . . . Luigi Giacosi
Format . . . . 35 mm, black and white/normal
Running time . . . . approx. 94 Min.
First showing in Italy . . . . . . Sept. 11, 1954
Awards (among others): Golden Lion at the Ven-
ice Film Festival, two Nastri d'argento awards for
Best Film and Best Director, the New York Film
Critics' Award, and the Oscar for Best Foreign
Film.

Production

Director . . . . Federico Fellini
Idea . . . . . . Federico Fellini, Tullio Pinelli
Screenplay . . . Federico Fellini, Ennio Flaiano,
. . . . Tullio Pinelli
Photographic direction . . . . Otello Martellini
Camera . . . . Roberto Girardi
Editing . . . . Leo Catozzo
Music . . . . Nino Rota
Scenery . . . . Mario Ravasco
Costumes . . . . Margherita Marinari
Sound . . . . A. Calpini

Cast

Role	Actor
Gelsomina	Giulietta Masina
Zampanò	Anthony Quinn
The tightrope walker	Richard Basehart
The ringmaster	Aldo Silvani
The widow	Marcella Rovere
The young nun	Lidia Venturini
	and many others

The Swindle

Original title . . . . Il bidone
Year of origin 1955
Production companies . . . . . Titanus (Rome),
. . . . S.G.C. (Paris)
Producer . . . . Mario de Vecchi
Executive producer . . . . Giuseppe Colizzi
Format . . . . 35 mm, black and white/normal

Running time . . . . approx. 104 Min.
First showing in Italy . . . . Sept. 10, 1955

Production
Director . . . . Federico Fellini
Idea . . . . Federico Fellini
Screenplay . . . Federico Fellini, Ennio Flaiano,
. . . . Tullio Pinelli
Photographic direction . . . . . . Otello Martelli
Camera . . . . Roberto Girardi
Editing . . . . Mario Serandrei, Giuseppe Vari
Music . . . . Nino Rota
Scenery . . . . Dario Cecchi
Costumes . . . . Dario Cecchi
Sound . . . . Giovanni Rossi

Cast
Role	Actor
Augusto	Broderick Crawford
Roberto	Franco Fabrizzi
Picasso	Richard Basehart
Iris, Picasso's wife . . .	Giulietta Masina
"Baron" Vargas	Giacomo Gabrielli
Rinaldo	Alberto De Amicis
Susanna	Sue Ellen Blake
Patrizia	Loretta De Luca
Luciana	Xenia Valderi
Marisa	Iene Cefaro
Stella Fiorina	Maria Zanoli
Bevilacqua	Ettore Bevilacqua
. . . .	and many others

The Nights of Cabiria
Original title . . . . Le notti di Cabiria
Year of origin 1957
Production companies . . De Laurentiis (Rome),
. . . . Les Films Marceau (Paris)
Producer . . . . Dino De Laurentiis
Executive producer . . . . Luigi De Laurentiis
Format . . . . . 35 mm, black and white/normal
Running time . . . . approx. 110 Min.
First shown at Cannes Film Festival

Sept. 9, 1957

Production
Director . . . . Federico Fellini
Idea . . . . Federico Fellini
Screenplay . . . Federico Fellini, Ennio Flaiano,
. . . . Tullio Pinelli
Dialogue in Roman dialect by

Pier Paolo Pasolini
Camera . . . . Aldo Tonti
Editing . . . . Leo Catozzo
Music . . . . Nino Rota
Scenery . . . . Piero Gherardi
Costumes . . . . Piero Gherardi
Sound . . . . Roy Mangano

Cast
Role	Actor
Cabiria	Giulietta Masina
Oscar D'Onofrio	François Périer
Wanda	Franca Marzi
Alberto Lazzari	Amedeo Nazzari
Jessy	Dorian Gray
The monk	Polidor
The hypnotist	Aldo Silvani
The cripple	Mario Passante
. . . .	and many others

La Dolce Vita
Original title . . . . La dolce vita
Year of origin 1960
Production companies
. . . . Riama Films (Rome), Cinecittà,
. . . . Pathé Consortium Cinéma (Paris)
Producers . . . Angelo Rizzoli, Giuseppe Amato
Executive producer . . . . Franco Magli
Format . . . . 35 mm, black and white/normal
Running time . . . . approx. 178 Min.
First showing in Italy . . . . . . Feb. 5, 1960
Awards (among others): Three Nastri d'argento
awards for Best Idea, Best Actor, Best Architect

Production
Director . . . . Federico Fellini
Idea . . . . Federico Fellini, Tullio Pinelli,
. . . . Ennio Flaiano
Screenplay . . . Federico Fellini, Ennio Flaiano,
. . . . Tullio Pinelli, Brunello Rondi
Photographic director . . . . . Otello Martelli
Camera . . . . Arturo Zavattini
Editing . . . . Leo Catozzo
Music . . . . Nino Rota
Scenery . . . . Piero Gherardi
Costumes . . . . Piero Gherardi
Sound . . . . Agostino Moretti, Oscar Di Santo

Cast
Role	Actor
Marcello Rubini	Marcello Mastroianni
Paparazzo	Walter Santesso
Maddalena	Anouk Aimée
Marcello's wife	Yvonne Furneaux
Sylvia	Anita Ekberg
Robert	Lex Barker
Steiner	Alain Cuny
Steiner's wife	Renée Longarini
Marcello's father	Annibale Ninchi
Fanny	Magali Noël
Nadia	Nadia Gray
Rock'n'Roll singer	Adriano Celentano
. . . .	and many others

The Temptation of Dr. Antonio
Original title . . Le tentazioni del dottor Antonio
Second episode from Boccacio 70 (Directors of the
other episodes: Vittorio De Sica, Mario Monicelli,
Luchino Visconti)
Year of origin 1962
Production companies . . Concordia Campagna
. . . . . . Cinematografica and Cineriz (Rome),
. . . . Francinex and Gray Films (Paris)
Producers . . . . Carlo Ponti, Ugo Tucci,
. . . . Sante Chimirri, Antonio Cervi
Format . 35 mm, widescreen Technicolor, 1 : 1,85
Length of episode . . . . . . approx. 60 Min.
First showing in Italy . . . . . . Feb. 22, 1962

Production
Director . . . . Federico Fellini
Idea . . . . . . Federico Fellini, Ennio Flaiano,
. . . . Tullio Pinelli
Screenplay . . . Federico Fellini, Ennio Flaiano,
. . . . Tullio Pinelli

Photographic direction . . . . . Otello Martelli
Camera . . . . Arturo Zavattini
Editing . . . . Leo Catozzo
Music . . . . Nino Rota
Scenery . . . . Piero Zuffi

Cast
Role	Actor
Doctor Antonio Mazzuolo . .	Peppino De Filippo
Anita, the woman from the poster	
	Anita Ekberg
Commendatore La Pappa	Antonio Acqua
Antonio's sister	Della Nora
The little girl	Eleonora Maggi
. . . .	and many others

8½
Original title . . . . Otto e mezzo
Year of origin 1963
Production companies . . . . Cineriz (Rome),
. . . . Francinex (Paris)
Producer . . . . Angelo Rizzoli
Executive producers . . . . . Nello Meniconi,
. . Alessandro von Normann, Clemente Fracassi
Format . . . 35 mm, black and white/widescreen
Running time . . . . approx. 141 Min.
First showing in Italy . . . . . . Feb. 15, 1963
Awards (among others): First Prize at the Moscow
Film Festival, seven Nastri d'argento awards for
Best Director, Best Producer, Best Subject, Best
Screenplay, Best Music, Best Photography, and
Best Supporting Actress, the New York Film Cri-
tics' Award, two Oscars for Best Foreign Film and
Best Costumes in a Black and White Film.

Production
Director . . . . Federico Fellini
Idea . . . . . . Federico Fellini, Ennio Flaiano
Screenplay . . . Federico Fellini, Ennio Flaiano,
. . . . Tullio Pinelli, Brunello Rondi
Photographic direction . . . Gianni Di Venanzo
Camera . . . . Pasquale De Santis
Editing . . . . Leo Catozzo
Music . . . . Nino Rota
Scenery . . . . Piero Gherardi
Costumes . . . . Piero Gherardi
Sound . . . Mario Faraoni, Alberto Bartolomei

Cast
Role	Actor
Guido	Marcello Mastroianni
Carla	Sandra Milo
Luisa	Anouk Aimée
Claudia	Claudia Cardinale
Rossella	Rossella Falk
Gloria	Barbara Steele
Mezzabotta	Mario Pisu
Pace	Guido Alberti
Guido's father	Annibale Ninchi
Guido's mother	Giuditta Rissone
The Cardinal	Tito Masini
Saraghina	Edra Gale
The producer	Mario Conocchia
The intellectual	Jean Rougeul
Maurice	Ian Dallas
A clown	Polidor
. . . .	and many others

Juliet of the Spirits

Original title	Giulietta degli spiriti
Year of production	1965
Production companies	Federiz (Rome),
	Francoriz (Paris), Eichberg-Film
Producer	Angelo Rizzoli
Executive producer	Mario Basili,
	Alessandro von Normann
Format	35 mm, widescreen/Technicolor
Running time	approx. 140 Min.
First showing in Italy	Oct. 22, 1965

Production

Director	Federico Fellini
Idea	Federico Fellini, Tullio Pinelli
Screenplay	Federico Fellini, Ennio Flaiano,
	Tullio Pinelli, Brunello Rondi
Photographic direction	Gianni Di Venanzo
Camera	Pasquale De Santis
Editing	Ruggero Mastroianni
Music	Nino Rota
Scenery	Piero Gherardi
Costumes	Piero Gherardi
Sound	Mario Faraoni, Mario Morici

Cast

Role	Actor
Julia	Giulietta Masina
Giorgio	Mario Pisu
Susy, Iris, Fanny	Sandra Milo
Valentina	Valentina Cortese
The mother	Caterina Boratto
Sylvia	Sylvia Koscina
Adele	Luisa Della Noce
José	José Luis de Vilallonga
Dolores	Silvana Jachino
The grandfather	Lou Gilbert
Bhishma	Valeska Gert
The psychoanalyst	Anne Francine
The detective	Alberto Plebani
	and many others

Never Bet the Devil your Head

Original title	Toby Dammit
Third episode from	Tre passi nel delirio
(Directors of the other episodes	Louis Malle,
	Roger Vadim)
Year of origin	1968
Production companies	P.E.A. (Rome),
	Les Films Marceau (Paris), Cocinor (Paris)
Producer	Alberto Grimaldi
Executive producer	Tommaso Sagone
Format	
	35 mm, widescreen/Eastmancolor, 1:1,85
Length of episode	approx. 40 Min.
First showing Cannes Film Festival	
	May 17, 1968
First showing in Italy	July 1968

Production

Director	Federico Fellini
Idea	Based on the short story by Edgar
	Allan Poe "Never bet the devil your head –
	A tale with a moral."
Screenplay	Federico Fellini,
	Bernardino Zapponi
Photographic direction	Giuseppe Rotunno
Camera	Giuseppe Maccari
Editing	Ruggero Mastroianni
Music	Nino Rota

Scenery	Piero Tosi
Costumes	Piero Tosi
Special effects	Joseph Nathanson

Cast

Role	Actor
Toby Dammit	Terence Stamp
The priest	Salvo Randone
The actress	Antonia Pietrosi
The old actor	Polidor
The devil's girl	Marina Yaru
Television moderator	Anna Tonietti
First director	Fabrizio Angeli
Second interviewer	Paul Cooper
	and many others

Fellini – A Director's Notebook

Original title	Block-Notes di un regista
Year of production	1969
Production company	National Broadcasting
	Company
Producer	Peter Goldfarb
Executive producer	Lamberto Pippia
Format	16 mm, Eastmancolor/normal
Running time	approx. 60 Min.
First showing	NBC-TV, USA, April 11, 1969

Production

Director	Federico Fellini
Idea	Federico Fellini, Bernardino Zapponi
Screenplay	
	Federico Fellini, Bernardino Zapponi
Photographic direction	Pasquale De Santis
Editing	Ruggero Mastroianni
Music	Nino Rota

Cast

Federico Fellini, Marcello Mastroianni, Giulietta Masina, Prof. Genius, Marina Boratto, Caterina Boratto, David Mausell, Cesarino, Gasparino, Lina Alberti, Alvaro Vitali and many others

Fellini's Satyricon

Original title	Fellini Satyricon
Year of origin	1969
Production companies	P.E.A. (Rome),
	Les Productions Artistes Associés (Paris)
Producer	Alberto Grimaldi
Executive producer	Roberto Cocco
Format	35 mm, Technicolor/Panavision
Running time	approx. 138 Min.
First showing in Italy	Sept. 4, 1969

Production

Director	Federico Fellini
Idea	Based on the novel of the same name
	by Petronius Arbiter
Screenplay	
	Federico Fellini, Bernardino Zapponi
Photographic direction	Giuseppe Rotunno
Camera	Giuseppe Maccari
Editing	Ruggero Mastroianni
Music	Nino Rota together with
	Ilhan Mimaroglu, Tod Dockstader
	and Andrew Rudin
Scenery	Danilo Donati
Camera	Danilo Donati
Sound	Oscar De Arcangelis

Cast

Role	Actor
Encolpius	Martin Potter
Asyltus	Hiram Keller
Gitone	Max Born
Trimalchio	Mario Romagnoli
Vernacchio	Fanfulla
Furtunata	Magali Noël
Habbinas	Giuseppe San Vitale
Lichas	Alain Cuny
The suicide	Joseph Wheeler
The suicide's wife	Lucia Bose
Fortunata's friend	Danika La Loggia
Robber of the hermaphrodite	Hylethe Adolphe
Nymphomanin	Sibilla Sedat
	and many others

The Clowns

Original title	I clowns
Year of production	1970
Production companies	RAI TV. (Rome),
	O.R.T.F. (Paris), Bavaria Film (Munich),
	Compagnia Leone Cinematografica (Rome)
Producers	Elio Scardamaglia, Ugo Guerra
Executive producer	Lamberto Pippia
Format	35 mm, Technicolor/normal
Running time	approx. 95 Min.
First showing in Italy	Dec. 25, 1970
in cinemas	Dec. 26, 1970

Production

Director	Federico Fellini
Idea	Federico Fellini
Screenplay	Federico Fellini,
	Bernardino Zapponi
Photographic direction	Dario Di Palma
Camera	Blasco Giurato
Editing	Ruggero Mastroianni
Music	Nino Rota
Scenery	Renzo Gronchi
Camera	Danilo Donati
Sound	Alberto Bartolomei

Cast

Federico Fellini, Anita Ekberg, Nando Orfei, Franco Migliorini, Jean-Baptiste Thierre, Pierre Etaix, Gustave Fratelli, Annie Fratellini, Maya Morin, Lina Alberti, Alvaro Vitali, Gasperino, Tristan Rèmy, Liana, Rinaldo as well as the clowns: Billi, Tino Scotti, Fanfulla, Carlo Rizzo, Fredo Pistoni, Furia, Sbarra, Carini, Terzo, Vingelli, Fumagalli, Zerbinati, Reder, Valentini, Merli, the 4 Colombaioni, Martana, Maggio, Janigro, Maunsell, Peverello, Sorentino, Valdemaro, Bevilacqua, Alex, Père Loriot, Maiss, Bario, Ludo, Charlie Rivel, Nino, Rhum …

Fellini's Roma

Original title	Roma
Year of production	1972
Production companies	
	Ultra Films S.P.A. (Rome),
	Les Productions Artistes Associés (Paris)
Producer	Turi Vasile
Executive producer	Lamberto Pippia
Format	35 mm, Technicolor/widescreen
Running time	approx. 120 Min.

First showing . . . . Cannes Film Festival,
. . . . March 14, 1972
First showing in Italy . . . . . . March 16, 1972

Production

Director . . . . Federico Fellini
Idea . . . Federico Fellini, Bernardino Zapponi
Screenplay . . . . Federico Fellini,
. . . . Bernardino Zapponi
Photographic direction . . . . Giuseppe Rotunno
Camera . . . . Giuseppe Maccari
Editing . . . . Ruggero Mastroianni
Music . . . . Nino Rota
Scenery . . . . Danilo Donati
Costumes . . . . Danilo Donati
Sound . . . . Renato Cadueri

Cast

Federico Fellini, Marcello Mastroianni, Anna
Magnani, Gore Vidal, Alberto Sordi

Role	Actor
Fellini as an 18 year old	Peter Gonzales
Fellini as a child	Stefano Majore
Princess	Pia De Dores
Cardinal Ottaviani . . .	Renato Giovannoli
Young prostitute	Fiona Florence
Companion in underground shaft	Marne
. . . .	Maitland
Script-girl	Britta Barnes
Variety dancer	Libero Frissi
Fred Astaire-imitator	Alvaro Vitali
. . . .	and many others

Amarcord

Original title	Amarcord
Year of origin	1973
Production companies .	F.C Produzioni (Rome),
. . . .	P.E.C.F. (Paris)
Producer	Franco Cristaldi
Executive producer	Lamberto Pippia
Format	35mm, Technicolor/widescreen
Running time	approx. 127 Min.
First showing in Italy	Dec. 18, 1973
Awards (among others)	Oscar for Best
. . . .	Foreign Film

Production

Director . . . . Federico Fellini
Idea . . . . Federico Fellini
Screenplay . , ... Federico Fellini,
. . . . Bernardino Zapponi
Photographic direction . . . . Giuseppe Rotunno
Camera . . . . Giuseppe Maccari
Editing . . . . Ruggero Mastroianni
Music . . . . Nino Rota
Scenery . . . . Danilo Donati
Costumes . . . . Danilo Donati
Sound . . . . Oscar De Arcangelis

Cast

Role	Actor
Titta	Bruno Zanin
Titta's mother	Pupella Maggio
Titta's father	Armando Brancia
Titta's uncle	Nando Orfei
Titta's grandfather	Peppino Janigro
The housemaid	Carla Mora
Oliva	Stefano Proietti

Naso	Alvaro Vitali
Ovo	Bruno Scagnetti
Gigliozzi	Bruno Lenzi
Il ciccio	Fernando De Felice
Candela	Francesco Vona
The tobacco vendor .	Maria Antonietta Beluzzi
Grandisca	Magali Noël
. . . .	and many others

Fellini's Casanova

Original title . . .	Il Casanova di Federico Fellini
Year of origin	1976
Production company	P.E.A. (Rome)
Producer	Alberto Grimaldi
Executive producer	Lamberto Pippia
Format	35 mm, Technicolor/widescreen
Running time	approx. 170 Min.
First showing in Italy	Dec. 11, 1976
Awards . .	The Oscar for Best Costume Designer

Production

Director . . . . Federico Fellini
Idea . . . . Based on the memories of
. . . . Giacomo Casanova
Screenplay . . . . Federico Fellini,
. . . . Bernardino Zapponi
Photographic direction . . . . Giuseppe Rotunno
Camera . . . . Massimo Di Venanzo
Editing . . . . Ruggero Mastroianni
Music . . . . Nino Rota
Scenery . . . . Danilo Donati
Costumes . . . . Danilo Donati
Sound . . . . Oscar De Arcangelis

Cast

Role	Actor
Casanova	Donald Sutherland
Maddalena	Margaret Clementi
Annamaria	Clarissa Mary Roll
Madame D'Urfé	Cecily Browne
Marcolina	Claretta Algranti
Henriette	Tina Aumont
Giselda	Daniela Gatti
Du Bois	Daniel Emilfork Berenstein
Lord Talow	John Karlsen
Casanova's brother	Nicolas Smith
Casanova's mother	Marie Marquet
Mechanical woman	Lede Lojodice
Prince del Brando	Hans van den Hoek
. . . .	and many others

Orchestra Rehearsal

Original title	Prova d'orchestra
Year of production	1979
Production companies .	Daime Cinematografica
. . . .	S.P.A. and RAI-TV (Rome),
. . . .	Albatros Produktions GmbH (Munich)
Executive producer	Lamberto Pippia
Format	35 mm, Technicolor/normal
Running time	approx. 70 Min.
First showing in Italy	Feb. 22, 1979

Production

Director . . . . Federico Fellini
Idea . . . . . Federico Fellini, Brunello Rondi
Screenplay . . . Federico Fellini, Brunello Rondi

Photographic direction	Giuseppe Rotunno
Editing	Ruggero Mastroianni
Music	Nino Rota
Scenery	Dante Ferretti
Costumes	Gabriella Pescucci

Cast

Role	Actor
Conductor	Balduin Baas
Harpist	Clara Colocimo
Pianist	Elisabeth Labi
Contrabassist	Ronaldo Bonacchi
Cellist	Ferdinando Villela
Tuba	Giovanni Javarone
First violin	David Muashell
Second violin	Francesco Aluigi
Oboe	Andy Miller
Flautist	Sybyl Mostert
Trumpet	Franco Mazzieri
Trombonist	Daniele Pagani
Violist	Luigi Uzzo
Clarinetist	Cesare Martignone
Music transcriber	Umberto Zuanelli
Unionist	Claudio Ciocca
Violist	Angelica Hansen
Violist	Heinz Kreuger

With the voice of Federico Fellini as interviewer . . .

La Città delle Donne

Original title	Città delle donne
Year of production	1980
Production companies	Opera Film
. . . .	Produzzioni (Rome), Gaumont (Paris)
Producer	Franco Rosselini
Executive producer	Lamberto Pippia,
. . . .	Francesco Orefici
Format	35 mm, Technicolor/widescreen
Running time	approx. 145 Min.
First showing	
. . . . .	Cannes Film Festival, May 19, 1980
First showing in Italy	1980

Production

Director . . . . Federico Fellini
Idea . . . . Federico Fellini
Screenplay . . . . Federico Fellini,
. . . . Bernardino Zapponi
Photographic direction . . . . Giuseppe Rotunno
Camera . . . . Gianni Fiori
Editing . . . . Ruggero Mastroianni
Music . . . . Dante Ferretti
Costumes . . . . Gabriella Pescucci
Sound . . . . Tommaso Quattrini,
. . . . Paul Marie Lorrain

Cast

Role	Actor
Snaporaz	Marcello Mastroianni
His wife	Anna Prucnal
Dottore Sante Katzone	Ettore Manni
The woman from the train . . .	Bernice Stegers
The motorcyclist	Iole Silvani
Donatella	Donatella Famiani
Ollio	Fiametta Baralla
Commandant	Catherine Carrel
Katzone's ten-thousandth lover .	Carla Terlizzi
The old woman	Mara Ciukleva
. . . .	and many, many other women

And the Ship Sails On

Original title	E la nave va
Year of origin	1983
Production companies	RAI-TV,
. . . .	Vides Produzione (Rome),
. . . .	Gaumont (Paris)
Producer	Franco Cristaldi
Executive producer	Lucio Orlandini
Format	35 mm, Technicolor/widescreen
Running time	approx. 132 Min.
First showing in Italy	Sept. 10, 1983

Production

Director	Federico Fellini
Idea	Federico Fellini, Tonino Guerra
Screenplay . . .	Federico Fellini, Tonino Guerra
Photographic direction	Giuseppe Rotunno
Editing	Ruggero Mastroianni
Music	Gianfranco Plenizio
Song lyrics	Andrea Zanzotto
Scenery	Dante Ferretti
Costumes	Maurizio Millenotti

Cast

Role	Actor
Orlando	Freddie Jones
Ildebranco Cuffari	Barbara Jefford
Aureliano Fuciletto	Victor Poletti
Sir Reginald Dongby	Peter Cellier
Lady Violet Dongby	Norma West
Teresa Valegnani	Elisa Mainardi
Maestro Albertini	Paolo Paolini
Dorothea	Sarah Jane Varley
Grand Duke	Fiorenzo Serra
Princess Lerinia	Pina Bausch
Conte Di Bassano	Pasquale Zito
Ines Ruffo Saltini	Linda Polan
Prime Minister	Philip Locke
Ricotin	Jonathan Cecil
U. O. Ziloev . . . . , , ,	Maurice Barrier
Sabatino Lepori	Fred Williams
Producer	Elisabeth Kaza
Chief of police	Colin Higgins
First Maestro Rubetti	Umberto Zuanelli
Second Maestro Rubetti	Vittorio Zarfati
. . . .	and many others

Ginger and Fred

Original title	Ginger e Fred
Year of origin	1985
Production companies .	Stella Film and Bibo TV
. . . .	together with Anthea (Munich),
. . . .	P.E.A. (Rome), Revcom (Paris)
Producer	Alberto Grimaldi
Executive producers .	Walter Massi, Gianfranco
. Codutti, Roberto Mannoni, Raymond Leplont
Format	35 mm, Colour
Running time	approx. 125 Min.
First showing	Paris, Jan. 13, 1986

Production

Director	Federico Fellini
Idea	Federico Fellini, Tonino Guerra
Screenplay . . .	Federico Fellini, Tonino Guerra,
. . . .	in association with Tullio Pinelli
Photographic direction	Tonino Delli Colli,
. . . .	Ennio Guarnieri
Camera	Aldo Marchiori, Carlo Tafani,

. . . .	Giovanni Fiore
Editing . .	Ruggero Mastroianni, Nino Baragli,
. . . .	Ugo De Rossi
Music	Nicola Piovani
Scenery	Dante Ferretti
Costumes	Danilo Donati

Cast

Role	Actor
Ginger alias Amelia	Giulietta Masina
Fred alias Pippo	Marcello Mastroianni
Showmaster	Franco Fabrizzi
Admiral	Friedrich von Ledebur
Transvestite	Augusto Poderosi
Assistant director	Martin Maria Blau
Industrialist	Friedrich von Thun
Pater Gerolamo	Jacques Henri Lartigue
Toto	Toto Mignone
Author	Ezio Marano
Productions secretary	Antonio Iuori
Journalist	Barbara Scoppa
Journalist	Elisabetta Flumeri
The woman who hears voices .	Ginestra Spinola
Productions secretary	Stefania Marini
Mafioso	Francesco Casale
. . . .	and many others

Intervista

Original title	Intervista
Year of origin	1987
Production companies . . .	Aljosha Produktion
. . . . .	Company with Fernlyn, RAI-TV
. . . .	and also Cinecittà
Producer	Ibrahim Moussa
Executive producer	Pietro Notariannik,
. . . .	Michele Janczarek
Format	35 mm, Colour
Running time	approx. 107 Min.
First showing	
. . . .	Cannes Film Festival, May 18, 1987
First showing in Italy	October 1987
Awards: Cannes Film Festival Special Award, Audience Award, and Grand Prize at the Moscow Film Festival	

Production

Director	Federico Fellini
Idea	Federico Fellini
Screenplay	Federico Fellini,
. . . .	Gianfranco Angelucci
Photographic direction	Tonino Delli Colli
Editing	Nino Baragli
Music	Nicola Piovani
Scenery	Danilo Donati
Costumes	Danilo Donati

Cast

Role	Actor
The journalist	Sergio Rubini
Antonella	Antonella Ponziani
The bride	Lara Wendel
The diva	Paola Liguori
Nadia	Nadia Ottavani
. . . .	as well as Federico Fellini, Danilo Donati, Tonino Delli Colli, Maurizio Mein, Pietro Notarianni, Anita Ekberg, Marcello Mastroianni and many others	

La Voce della Luna

Original title	La voce della Luna
Year of origin	1989/90
Production companies	C. G. Group Tiger
. . . . .	Cinematografica – Cinemax, R.A.I. –
. . . . . .	Radiotelevisione Italiana
Producers . . .	Mario and Vittorio Cecchi Gori
Executive Producers	Bruno Altissimi
. . . .	and Claudio Saraceni
Format	35 mm, Colour
Running time	approx. 120 Min.
First showing in Italy	Jan. 31, 1990

Production

Director	Federico Fellini
Idea	Based loosely
. . . . . .	on the novel Il Poema dei Lunatici
. . . .	by Ermanno Cavazzoni
Screenplay	Federico Fellini,
. . . .	Tullio Pinelli, Ermanno Cavazzoni
Photographic direction . . .	Tonino Delli Colli
Editing	Nino Baragli
Music	Nicola Piovani
Scenery	Dante Ferretti
Costumes	Maurizio Millenotti

Cast

Role	Actor
Salvini	Roberto Benigni
The Prefect Gonella	Paolo Villaggio
Aldina	Nadia Ottaviani
The "Locomotive"	Marisa Tomasi
The oboist	Sim
Aldina's sister	Syusy Blady
Nestore	Angelo Orlando
The journalist	Dario Ghirardi
The Brothers Micheluzzi	
. . . . . .	Dominique Chevalier,
. . . . .	Nigel Harris, Vito
The Duchess	Lorose Keller
. . . .	and many others

142

The author wishes to thank:

Gudrun Bießmann, Anke Blöcher, Kirsten Bollmann (Warner Home Video), Werner Büg, Gabriele Conze, Tilmann P. Gangloff, Josef Garncarz, Rudolf Hartmann, Rainer Hassert, Jutta Heselmann, Ursula Kotschi (United International Pictures/Twentieth Century Fox), Margarete Langen, Françoise Lemporte (Colosseum Schallplatten), Patrick Löffler, Helmut Merker, Karsten Prüßmann, Armin Schneider (Warner Bros. Film), Madelonne von Schrenck, Jane Smith (Virgin Rekords), Silke Svatunek, Eva Tembrink, Julia Tethi, Rudy Tjio (Prokino), Doris Wiesental (BMG Ariola), Meinolf Zurhorst

as well as:

Concorde-Film, CBS-Fox-Video, Deutsches Video Institut e. V., EMI Electrola, Institut für Theater-, Film- und Fernsehwissenschaften Köln, Österreichisches Filmmuseum Wien, Rough Trade Records, Tobis Filmkunst und Taurus Beta Video.

Originals for reproduction were received from:

Elisabetta Catalano, Rome:
Frontcover, 56 top, 56 bottom, 61 top, 61 bottom, 62 top, 62 bottom, 64 top, 64 bottom, 65 top, 65 bottom, 66 top, 66 bottom, 67, 68/69, 70 top, 70 bottom, 71, 72 top, 72 bottom.
Archiv Robert Fischer, Munich:
10, 11 top, 11 bottom, 12 top, 12 bottom, 13, 14, 15, 22, 27, 28, 30, 31 top, 31 bottom, 32, 33, 34, 35 top, 36, 41, 42 top, 42 bottom, 43, 44, 49, 50, 51, 52 top, 52 bottom, 53, 55 top, 55 bottom, 58/59, 59, 60 top, 60 bottom, 96, 97, 98 1., 2., 3. from top, 99 2., 3., 4. from top, 100, 101, 102, 103 top, 103 bottom, 104 top, 104 bottom, 105, 107, 108, 109, 110 top, 110 bottom, 111, 113, 114 top, 114 bottom, 116, 117, 119, 120 top left, 122 top, 122 bottom, 124, 125
Interfoto – Pressebild – Agentur, Munich:
6, 16 top, 16 bottom, 17, 19, 20, 23 top, 23 bottom, 25, 26 top, 26 bottom, 35 bottom, 38, 39 top, 39 bottom, 54, 91, 93, 94, 95 top, 95 bottom, 129.
Archiv Dr. Karkosch, Gilching:
37, 45, 46, 47.
Enrica Scalfari/AGF, Rome:
Backcover, 85, 86, 86/87, 88 top, 88 bottom, 89, 90.
All other illustrations originate from the archives of the publisher and the author:

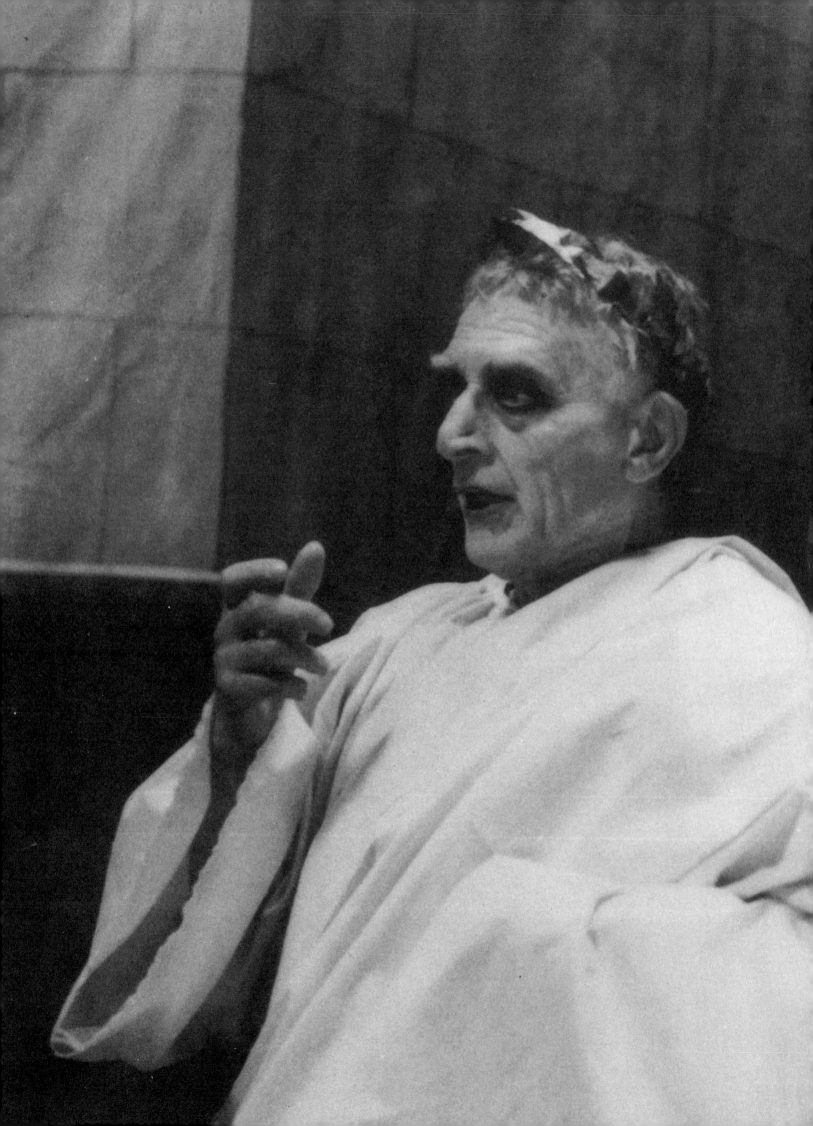